HUMAN RESOURCE MANAGEMENT
IN CONTEXT

HELEN NEWELL AND HARRY SCARBROUGH

HUMAN RESOURCE MANAGEMENT IN CONTEXT

A CASE STUDY APPROACH

palgrave

First published 2002 by
PALGRAVE
Houndmills, Basingstoke, Hampshire RG21 6XS and
175 Fifth Avenue, New York, N.Y. 10010
Companies and representatives throughout the world

PALGRAVE is the new global academic imprint of
St. Martin's Press LLC Scholarly and Reference Division and
Palgrave Publishers Ltd (formerly Macmillan Press Ltd).

ISBN 0–333–92135–6 hardback
ISBN 0–333–92136–4 paperback

This book is printed on paper suitable for recycling and
made from fully managed and sustained forest sources.

A catalogue record for this book is available
from the British Library.

Library of Congress Cataloging-in-Publication Data

Human resource management in context : a case study
approach / [edited by] Helen Newell and Harry Scarbrough.
      p. cm.
   Includes bibliographical references and index.
   ISBN 0–333–92135–6 (cloth)
    1. Personnel management. 2. Personnel management—Case
studies. 3. Personnel management—Great Britain. 4. Personnel
management—Great Britain—Case studies. I. Newell, Helen.
II. Scarbrough, Harry, 1955–

HF5549 .H788 2001
658.3—dc21   2001046159

Designed by
Claire Brodmann Book Designs, Lichfield, Staffs

Editing and origination by
Aardvark Editorial, Mendham, Suffolk

10 9 8 7 6 5 4 3 2 1
11 10 09 08 07 06 05 04 03 02

Printed in China

CONTENTS

1 INTRODUCTION

2 UNDERSTANDING HUMAN RESOURCE MANAGEMENT

3 ALCAN: MANAGING CHANGE

$\mathcal{L}$IST OF FIGURES AND TABLES

$\mathcal{F}$IGURES

$\mathcal{T}$ABLES

ACKNOWLEDGEMENTS

The authors and publishers would like to thank the following for permission to use copyright material:

Blackwell Publishers for Figure 2.2 from John Storey, *Developments in the Management of Human Resources*, 1992.

Every effort has been made to trace all the copyright holders but if any have been inadvertently overlooked the publishers will be pleased to make the necessary arrangements at the first opportunity.

ℕOTES ON THE CONTRIBUTORS

ELENA ANTONACOPOULOU is a Lecturer in Human Resources and Organisational Analysis at Manchester Business School. She was formerly a lecturer in Organisational Behaviour at Warwick Business School, University of Warwick. Her principal research interests concern individual and organisational learning and the effective management of change within organisations.

PAUL EDWARDS is the Director of the Industrial Relations Research Unit and Professor of Industrial Relations at the University of Warwick. He is co-author of five titles including *Attending to Work* (with Colin Whitston, 1993) and editor of *Industrial Relations: Theory and Practice in Britain* (1995, Oxford: Blackwell).

TONY EDWARDS is a Lecturer in the school of Human Resource Management at Kingston Business School, Kingston University. He was formerly a lecturer in Industrial Relations at Warwick Business School, University of Warwick. His research interests lie in the area of industrial relations in multinational companies, especially the diffusion of best practice.

SONIA LIFF is a Reader in Industrial Relations and Personnel Management at Warwick Business School, University of Warwick. Her research interests focus on women's employment experiences and the implementation of workplace equality policies. Other research and publications have been in the fields of technical change and employment and information systems for managing employee skills and the role of sites offering public access to computers and the internet in countering social exclusion from the information society.

CAROLINE LLOYD is a Warwick Research Fellow within Warwick Business School's ESRC-funded Research Centre SKOPE (Skills, Knowledge and Organisational Performance). Previously she was an ESRC Management Research Fellow with the Industrial Relations Research Unit at the University of Warwick. Her current research interests include the management of employees in the pharmaceutical and aerospace industries.

HELEN NEWELL is Lecturer in Industrial Relations and Personnel Management at Warwick Business School, University of Warwick. She is also a member of the Industrial Relations Research Unit. She has researched and written about employment relations in greenfield sites, the role of employee participation in workplace change and the impact of organisational change on the career patterns of middle managers.

HARRY SCARBROUGH is Research Director and Professor of Organisational Analysis, Leicester University Management Centre. Previously he was Senior Lecturer at Warwick Business School, University of Warwick. As well as work on the 'people management implications of lean production' for the Institute of Personnel and Development (see the 1998 IPD Report 'Getting Fit, Staying Fit'), his current research interests focus on knowledge management, networks and innovation and organisational responses to technological change.

KEITH SISSON is an Emeritus Professor of Industrial Relations at the University of Warwick and a former Director of the Industrial Relations Research Unit. He is one of the series editors of the Warwick Studies in Industrial Relations and author of several major books on industrial relations, including *Personnel Management in Britain* (with Stephen Bach) (2000, Oxford: Blackwell).

MARTYN WRIGHT is a Lecturer in Industrial Relations and Organisational Behaviour at Warwick Business School, University of Warwick and a member of the Industrial Relations Research Unit. His research interests lie in production systems and work organisation, workplace change and shop-floor bargaining.

*C*HAPTER ONE

INTRODUCTION

HELEN NEWELL AND HARRY SCARBROUGH

Human resource management (HRM) is defined here in simple terms as the management of people in organisations. In modern societies, with complex changes in the nature of work and technology, it is increasingly recognised that the effective and efficient production of goods and services requires more from employees than their passive compliance with managerial instructions. What is needed is their active commitment and initiative. Management of human resources can be seen to be as important for corporate success as the handling of any other management activities.

This text embodies a different, and, we believe, effective approach to the study of HRM. Most textbooks on HRM tend to be based either on theoretical discussions, or a relatively fixed menu of HRM tasks and functions. The latter would typically include tasks such as recruitment and selection, performance management, human resource planning and so on. Although the standard menu of HRM tasks still has a role to play in organisations, its usefulness is being steadily diminished by the shift away from traditional functional and hierarchical management structures towards process-based or even virtual forms. In a business process context, much of the responsibility for HRM issues is devolved to line management. HRM policy and practice is decoupled from the bureaucracy, to be determined by the prevailing pressures of a dynamic business environment, be that at an operational or strategic level.

For these reasons, we have moved away from these existing formats towards a case-based approach in which each case study illuminates a specific issue or theme which has wide relevance to management students. The rationale for the case-based approach can be presented briefly as follows:

- Much of the debate in HRM centres on the distinction between rhetoric and reality. We have privileged the latter, even at the expense of the neat ideal types of which HRM theorists are so fond.

- One of the reasons for the reality gap in much existing debate is to do with the importance of context for HRM practice.

Management actions which have a behavioural dimension – in other words, the bedrock of HRM practice – are not amenable to universal models based on rational actors. Behaviour is cued and enacted according to specific organisational, cultural and institutional contexts. The best way of understanding the context dependency of HRM practice is to show it in action through case examples.

- Research into HRM has consistently shown that the formal policies which organisations espouse are not always a good guide to the way they are implemented in practice. HRM policies often have unintended consequences which are not fully considered in the decision-making process. Case studies are an especially good medium for highlighting the contrast between policy and implementation, and for demonstrating the importance of unanticipated effects.

- To focus on the practice of HRM is not to dismiss the rhetoric as unimportant. Indeed, the symbolic order (cf. Tyson, 1995) which management seek to create within an organisation – the use of language and the manifestations of culture – has its own effects on employee behaviour. Again, however, the impact of the symbols is dependent on the way they are interpreted by specific employees within a specific context.

The advantages of case studies can easily be overstated of course. Although long established as a teaching method by Harvard Business School and others, the traditional business case study presents a highly selective view of organisational life. Viewing the world simply in terms of managerial problem-solving is a poor guide to the political and behavioural nuances of HRM practice. It follows that the case studies presented here are far removed from the Harvard model. Rather, each case is based on critically oriented empirical research, presenting an unvarnished, if necessarily abbreviated, account of a particular theme or issue. The accompanying briefing for each case serves to underline the contextual nature of HRM practice and the relevance of each case to wider HRM application.

This is, therefore, a collection of research-based case studies which report on real-life situations: they are neither anecdotes nor imaginary depictions. They are condensed insights generated out of in-depth research. All the case studies presented are taken from recent research undertaken by members of the Industrial Relations and Organisational Behaviour teaching group and members of the Industrial Relations Research Unit. They therefore reflect current issues in real organisations. They do not, however, represent an attempt to reproduce comprehensively the total range of situations to which HRM is relevant. Rather they represent a selection of those cases which raise important HR issues and which are both interesting and of current relevance in HRM.

In sequencing the case studies, our aim has been to analyse HRM at different levels, beginning with a focus on micro issues, enterprise or shop-floor relations (work organisation, pay, the introduction of new technology) and moving to a more macro focus, dealing with corporate HR policies (such as decisions about whether or not to become a 'learning organisation', whether to seek to develop partnership agreements, how to manage a diverse workforce) and finally to an international focus looking at HRM issues in a large multinational organisation.

While there are a number of human resource tasks common to most organisations (for example recruitment, pay and so on), it is also important to realise that HRM is about process – the ways in which organisations get things done through people. It is not just a bundle of techniques. For this reason the text is designed to develop your understanding and awareness of the main aspects of HRM as broadly defined. It does *not* provide a set of techniques which the manager can apply directly to her or his own organisation. The issues involved are too complex to permit the formulation of general laws or principles. Making sense of relations among workers, between managers and between management and the workforce is as much an art as a science. This helps to explain the bewildering succession of fads and fashions in this area, as publicists and consultants invent novel schemes for keeping employees happily productive. In fact there are no panaceas or universal recipes. For managers, there is ultimately no alternative to working out an approach to suit their own organisation's circumstances. The problems of doing so are eloquently underlined by the cases presented here.

*A*NALYSING CASE STUDIES

HRM involves a sensitive, multidisciplinary analysis of the issues. The problems encountered are rarely open to 'one best way' solutions. In most situations it is possible to argue persuasively for any of a range of different approaches. The test of analytical ability, then, is the extent to which the implications of the chosen policy have been thought through and the response to possible outcomes anticipated. Case studies provide the student with the opportunity to develop their ability to choose between and justify policy choices. This will enable students not only to connect their personal experience to general principles and arguments, but also to link analysis to practical situations.

Accompanying each case is a background briefing which helps to locate the case study against the backdrop of wider trends and concerns. This briefing provides pointers to the critical issues which emerge in each case, and also helps us to understand what is context specific or more general about those issues. Through a reading of the background briefing, the student should be able to develop a better analysis of the case itself, and an improved appreciation of the wider issues which it exemplifies.

There are many different approaches to analysing cases, depending on the preferences and learning style of the individual student. However, for most students the best approach normally involves following a 'step-by-step approach'. Addressing this to the student directly, we can identify the following major steps:

- Understanding the situation

- Defining the problem

- Generating and evaluating solutions

- Implementing solutions.

UNDERSTANDING THE SITUATION

This is perhaps the single most important stage in successfully analysing a case study and for this reason the majority of the second chapter has been spent in providing you with the necessary concepts and tools to do this. Each case study is also accompanied by a background briefing which locates it within wider themes and trends. Of course, understanding will also be enhanced through reading and rereading the case studies and trying to absorb the information. You need to work out what information is missing, what constitutes fact, and what is opinion. You also need to consider the situation from the different perspectives of the people involved in order to develop a full understanding of the case.

DEFINING THE PROBLEM

Often the specific questions that are asked will guide the student towards particular problem areas. However, you should not rely on this exclusively. You need to spend time identifying the problem(s). Problems are not always explicit, they may be implicit, becoming apparent only after the details of the case have been fully absorbed. They may be current problems or indications as to potential threats and opportunities, and problem areas may be interrelated. Finally, when you have formulated the problems, you should remember to provide supporting evidence from the case study. It is important to be able to identify what it was in the case study that led you to your conclusions.

When diagnosing the problem you should draw on your knowledge of the relevant literature. What problem is an organisation in this situation likely to suffer from, what problems have other organisations in this or similar situations suffered from, and what are the common problems within this particular area of HRM? Theoretical knowledge will be a major resource to draw upon, although your own knowledge and experience may also be relevant. This part of the case study process requires you to integrate your theoretical knowledge with your analysis of the practical situation.

The problems need to be analysed in terms of symptoms and causality. It can be useful at this stage to summarise your analysis in a short statement about the problems, with supporting evidence, and some attempt to prioritise problems, for example in terms of their importance to the organisation, urgency, and ease of solution.

GENERATING AND EVALUATING SOLUTIONS

There is rarely only one possible solution to a social science problem. You should try to be as creative as possible, while always bearing in mind what is feasible given the actual difficulties and complexities of the case and the context you have identified. Again, you will find the literature a useful source of material on what other companies have done in similar situations.

Try to predict the reaction to your proposed solutions, not only by managers but by other stakeholders in the organisation, particularly employees and their representative bodies. It is important to realise that line managers and HRM professionals may see your proposals in very different ways, so you need to think through what impact a solution will have on a whole range of individuals and groups throughout the organisation. You will find it useful to refer to the literature to predict any possible problems that may arise with your solutions. It is also important to clarify the criteria of choice between different solutions.

IMPLEMENTING SOLUTIONS

You should also be aware of the political processes at work in 'selling' your proposal. Who is going to have to be persuaded and convinced of what you say in order to make the proposal work? How are you going to persuade them? What types of argument are going to appeal to which groups/individuals? Who is likely to oppose your plans? What could you do about this? What is the cost of what you propose? What is the likely timetable of events? What will be the implications of change for different groups and individuals? Finally, you should always bear in mind whether the HRM department has the skills and/or power base to manage successfully the process and changes that you are advocating. If not, does your plan require the backing of another senior manager and who might this be?

REFERENCE

Tyson, S. (1995) *Human Resource Strategy: Towards a General Theory of HRM*. London: Pitman.

CHAPTER TWO

UNDERSTANDING HUMAN RESOURCE MANAGEMENT

HELEN NEWELL AND HARRY SCARBROUGH

*I*NTRODUCTION

This text is designed to improve the student's understanding of a wide range of HRM practices and issues. We aim to do this by grounding our discussion of HRM in the specific contexts and problems thrown up by real-life organisations. The case studies presented here, therefore, show the complex challenges facing managers and HRM practitioners in the current period. This is very different to the standard HRM text which offers a menu of HRM tasks which are assumed to be universally relevant. We have moved away from the idea that HRM involves a value-free and context-free set of tools and techniques. Instead, through our selection of cases we have sought to reflect the emerging problems and challenges which have brought about a perceived shift in the character and scope of HRM in contemporary organisations. This new agenda for HRM has been identified in a range of different research studies (Collinson et al., 1998; Scarbrough et al., 1998; Sparrow and Marchington, 1998). Drawing on these studies, we have identified the following themes as representing critical moments in the emergence of new challenges to HRM practice:

- *New forms of technology and organisation*
  The pressures of global competition and changing market contexts are driving the development of new ways of organising and controlling work. This demands new skills from employees and new HRM policies from employers. It also involves the ability to manage such change against the backdrop of the organisation's historical development, its legacy of employee relations, pay systems, and so on.

- *Changes in the employment relationship*
  One of the important developments accompanying the above-noted changes in the UK and many other countries has been the weakening of the role of trade unions and collective bargaining in shaping the employment relationship. While this

has arguably reduced the explicit level of employer–employee conflict, perceived trends towards job insecurity have threatened the implicit psychological contracts which used to be a feature of employment in many firms. New patterns of employee relations, including new reward systems, are being sought to alleviate the adverse consequences of some of these changes.

● *The drive for different kinds of flexibility*
The ability of firms to achieve new forms of partnership and commitment from employees is often linked to – and sometimes constrained by – a concern to bring about task and employment flexibility from these groups. In manufacturing, for example, the demands of lean production and the development of supply chain networks have created enormous pressures for work flexibility, pressures which are not always addressed through appropriate training and support systems (Collinson et al., 1998).

Table 2.1 Issues and themes addressed in the case studies

Key theme	Case study	Specific issues
New forms of technology and organisation	Alcan	Negotiation of teamworking under competitive pressures
	Multico	Employee involvement in technical change
Changes in the employment relationship	Accountco	HR planning in a small business
	London Borough	Partnership with unions in local government
	Pharmaco	Strategies for managing restructuring and job insecurity
	Telco	Strategies for managing employee diversity
The drive for different kinds of flexibility	Buildsoc	Linking pay to performance – problems of team-based payment
	Bankco	Development of a learning organisation through management development
	Engineering products	Impact of international integration on employees and work practices

The selection of cases presented here reflects these broad shifts in the context and nature of HRM practice. The specific issues of each case can be related to one or more of the themes making up the new agenda for HRM, as set out in Table 2.1.

DIMENSIONS OF CHANGE

As outlined above, the new agenda in HRM is essentially concerned with the tensions generated by the pursuit of change and competitiveness; the employer's desire to seek greater efficiency and flexibility being counterbalanced by the responses of employees and the implications for individual and group performance. Although there is a tendency to view these changes in one-dimensional terms – as all deriving from globalisation, for instance, or from the demands of IT – the reality is that change is a multidimensional and multilayered process, operating in different guises at firm, sector and society levels. In our cases, we can see change operating through a number of different forces and actors. In the following sections, we outline some of the most important aspects of change as viewed from this standpoint. They encompass the following aspects, each of which is considered in more detail below:

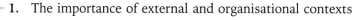

1. The importance of external and organisational contexts

2. The links between business strategy and HRM strategy

3. The role of management in HRM

4. Patterns of employment

5. The gap between HRM policy and practice.

THE IMPORTANCE OF EXTERNAL AND INTERNAL ORGANISATIONAL CONTEXTS

As we have already commented, in HRM there is rarely a 'one best way' solution to problems because of the importance of both the organisation's external and internal context. Analysing the context within which the organisation operates is fundamental to understanding what is appropriate and achievable in terms of future action.

THE EXTERNAL CONTEXT

The Political and Economic Context

The action of companies will partly be determined by the broad character of the political and economic environment. In the UK, the Labour government has undertaken a major review both of its policies (around the central theme of a 'stakeholder' society and the social responsibility of industry) and its relationship to the trade union movement. However, an equally important development in the political environment, so far as employment is concerned, has been the development of the European Union with its 'social democratic' ideology based on social partnership between government, capital and labour, which has had a substantial impact on legislation in member countries. The impact of this development on employee involvement and in particular attitudes towards trade unions is discussed in relation to the development of partnership agreements in Chapter 7.

In terms of economic factors, in general whether the economy is growing or is in recession will affect decisions about what is appropriate behaviour. Over and above this, an understanding of the action of different companies in different countries can be gained through knowledge of the different systems of corporate ownership and control. There are two main contrasting systems, an Anglo-American 'outsider system' and a Continental 'insider system'. The implications of these different systems for the way in which employees are managed are substantial and stem largely from a difference between *shareholder* and *stakeholder* interests in companies:

*U*nder outsider systems, the main control over the current management is exercised through the threat of takeover, the selling and buying of shareholdings. The outsider system is characterised by the power of the institutional shareholder. Companies operate within highly developed stock markets, where the emphasis is on short-term profits to provide share dividends in order to avoid hostile takeover. The emphasis is therefore on short-run financial returns and investors are more concerned with financial returns than with long-run industrial performance. As a result, a strong emphasis is placed upon monitoring and performance. Human resource policies are likely to be driven by the desire to minimise costs. This makes investment in employees, for example through training and development activities, less likely.

Under insider systems, internal supervision is carried out by stakeholders such as banks and employee representatives, rather than shareholders. The insider system is characterised by interlinked networks of corporate, institutional or family shareholdings and a financial system based on long-term bank credit. The stock market is much less well developed and there is therefore less exposure to hostile takeover than in the outsider system. Rather than being subject to short-term financial controls, organisations in insider systems are subject to operational controls. As a result employees are much more likely to be viewed as the organisation's source of competitive advantage, an asset to invest in.

(adapted from Marginson and Sisson, 1994)

Legal Context

A major difference between countries (and therefore between the way in which companies operate in different countries) is the extent to which employee relations and wider social and welfare issues are governed by the state. Legal issues set the scene for many aspects of the employment relationship. In many countries there are legal standards influencing decisions about recruitment and selection, training and development, employee rewards, discipline and equal opportunities. Some countries such as Britain have taken considerable steps to 'free up' the labour market, while other European countries have gone nowhere near so far. There are other substantial differences between countries. Both Australia and the USA, for example, have legally binding arbitration as a way of resolving industrial disputes which means that the whole concept of the contract of employment is fundamentally different. Indeed, not only does the legal context vary from country to country, the legal context within any particular country also changes over time. The impact of continuing European legislation on the UK is a good example of this phenomenon. A good source of up-to-date reports on European legislation, directives and debates is the European Industrial Relations Observatory (EIRO) which is based on a network of leading research institutes in each of the countries covered and coordinated by the European Foundation for the Improvement of Living and Working Conditions. Its aim is to collect, analyse and disseminate high quality, up-to-date information on key developments in industrial relations in Europe. You can access EIRO on http://www.eiro.eurofound.ie

Labour Markets

Countries differ markedly in the extent to which they have legal controls over the operation of labour markets. Within industries and occupations, changes in product markets and production methods can have a dramatic effect on particular labour markets over relatively short periods of time. The introduction of new technologies into both products and processes causes both types of change. Such changes can lead simultaneously to the unemployment of those whose skills are no longer required, and skill shortages where there are insufficient people with the skills needed for the jobs available. In Britain, the number of part-time, low-paid jobs, traditionally done by women, has grown, but so has the number of people looking for full-time employment. Thus, the problem for employers is not so much recruiting workers, but recruiting the right workers. There is no shortage of labour, but there is a shortage of labour with the right skills. Some hope of reducing this shortage, however, comes from demographic factors. In most countries, the workforce is growing. This growth comes in two ways; changes in the size of the working age population; and changes in the proportion of that population seeking work (participation or activity rates). The former is likely to be more significant in developing countries and the latter in developed ones.

Business Sector

There has been a growth in global markets with multinational companies operating on a worldwide basis, often using internal competition between units to encourage maximum performance. These developments, some commentators argue, suggest that a new kind of international organisation is needed; this is the 'transnational', epitomised by the development of a new 'managerial mentality', which seeks to build a learning and self-adaptive organisation that is both competitive and flexible on an international scale.

Alongside these broad international changes, there have been changes in the domestic industrial structure in many countries. In the UK, for example, there has been a rapid growth in the service sector. In 1971, 36% of all employees in Britain worked in manufacturing; by 1992 this had fallen to 21.4%. Conversely, in 1971, 52.6% of employees worked in service industries; by 1992 this had risen to nearly 71.6%. The severity of decline in manufacturing was particularly marked in coal, oil and gas extraction; metal manufacturing, ore and other mineral extraction; motor vehicles and parts; and textiles, leather, footwear and clothing. The strongest growth was in private sector services, the banking, insurance and financial sectors, hotels and catering and other services (personal, recreational and cultural) (*Employment Gazette*, 1992).

This long-term shift in employment from manufacturing to the service sector, as well as the greater technical sophistication of much of the surviving manufacturing, has resulted in a decline in manual jobs relative to non-manual jobs. This has had several knock-on effects. First, workplaces have tended to become increasingly polarised between those undertaking jobs requiring the skills of 'knowledge workers', and consequently high levels of education and training and those performing routinised, low-skill service jobs (check-out operators, shelf-fillers, fast-food operatives). Second, there are a greater number of women in the workforce, especially in service sector jobs, as it has become the norm for women to work, with only a minimal break for child-rearing. Third, due to demographic changes the workforce is becoming increasingly 'middle aged'.

Another area of change has been in the public sector. A substantial proportion of the national workforce in most industrialised countries is employed, directly or indirectly, by the government in the public sector. As well as such public services as health, education, police, fire and prisons, it may include public utility industries such as communications, transport, coal, electricity, gas and water and so on. Much of the public sector has, in the past, displayed managerial characteristics different from the private sector. The centralised nature of its policies, together with the responsibility for providing a 'public service' to the community, was often accompanied by complacency about employee motivation. There was also difficulty in applying market criteria, such as price, competition and profitability, to the pursuit of social needs.

In the UK, major changes in the public sector have been achieved first through privatisation of many previously nationalised industries, and, second, where public services remain, through the introduction of certain features of the market economy. These included, for example, the use of cash limits on spending coupled with the reduction of budgets (in real terms) and the introduction of performance appraisal and merit pay.

National Cultural Context

Although many of the most influential models of HRM have originated in the USA, their relevance to other countries is placed in question by growing recognition of cultural and institutional differences between nations. Although the proponents of globalisation stress the convergence of national cultures with the spread of global marketing, there are still enough cultural differences between nations to demand the careful adaptation of management practices.

The nature of these differences was highlighted originally by Hofstede's (1984) seminal research study of IBM employees around the world. This led to the identification of four dimensions of national culture which might be expected to affect business practice. From these he developed a set of cultural maps of the world by comparing the beliefs and values of employees within the subsidiaries of IBM and used these maps to show whether or not American management theories (about motivation, leadership and organisation for instance) were universally valid. He concluded that the theories reflected the particular cultural environment in which they were written – theories developed by middle-class American intellectuals reflected a national intellectual middle-class background. In other words, theories of motivation, developed by American authors, may well not apply in other countries.

The four dimensions along which Hofstede believed managers and employees differed across countries were power distance, uncertainty avoidance, individualism versus collectivism and masculinity versus femininity.

● *Power distance*
Hofstede defined power distance as the extent to which members of a society accept that power in institutions and organisations is distributed unequally. Large power distance is usually reflected in formal hierarchies where superior–subordinate relationships are clear. Hofstede found large power distance values for Latin countries (including both Latin Euro-

pean and Latin American countries) and for Asia and Africa, whereas Northern Europe scored low on this dimension.

- *Uncertainty avoidance*
  This dimension reflects a society's tolerance for uncertainty, ambiguity and conflict. A country with a high uncertainty avoidance value would seek to minimise this, for example through the provision of explicit rules and regulations. He found that the inclination to avoid uncertainty was strong in Latin America, Latin Europe, Mediterranean countries, Japan and Korea. Scores in Austria, Switzerland and Germany were also high. In contrast scores in Asia and Africa were lower.

- *Individualism versus collectivism*
  In countries where collectivism predominates the emphasis is on social ties or bonds between individuals so that people act as members of a cohesive group. In individualistic countries ties between individuals are loose and people are supposed to look after their own, rather than group interests. In general Hofstede found that wealthy countries scored high on individualism and poorer countries high on collectivism. One exception to this was Japan which showed quite strong collectivist features.

- *Masculinity versus femininity*
  This dimension refers to the dominant values in society. Where these values were about the work ethic, expressed in terms of money, achievement and recognition, Hofstede labelled them as masculine. Where these values were more concerned with people and quality of life, he labelled them as feminine. On this basis he found that Japan and Austria were highly masculine and the Scandinavian countries and the Netherlands highly feminine.

The work of Trompenaars (1993) also offers some insights into how national culture impacts on management practices. Like Hofstede, Trompenaars identified several dimensions as being important in determining how successful management practices would be in different national contexts. They are similar, but not identical, to those developed by Hofstede.

Universalism versus particularism

Universalism occurs where people believe that what is true and right can be applied in every circumstances – the same rule applies to everybody. In contrast, particularism occurs where it is believed that circumstances and relationships determine what is true and right, rather than an abstract rule. For example, 'I will deal with the situation in this way because this person is my friend, relative or person of importance to me'. This means that in universalistic cultures jobs will generally have a detailed job description, applicant's qualifications will be matched against the job's requirements and job performance will be measured against clearly specified standards. In particularist cultures there are unlikely to be any job descriptions or criteria for evaluating performance. Systems will be much more informal with the main criteria for appointment being a relationship with the owner of the firm or members of the owners' immediate family. Trompenaars's work revealed a distinction between West and East on this dimension. Most Western countries, for example the USA, the UK, Canada and Denmark, are classified as universalist and most Asian countries, for example Thailand, as particularist.

Individualism versus collectivism

In individualistic cultures the prime orientation is towards oneself, whereas in collective cultures the prime orientation is towards common goals and objectives. This, Trompenaars argues strongly, impacts on many aspects of management, but particularly negotiations, decision-making and motivation. Practices such as promotion for recognised achievements and pay for performance assume that individuals seek to be distinguished within their work group and that their colleagues approve of this happening. It also assumes that the contribution of any one member of the group can be easily identified and that no problems arise in singling her or him out for praise. These assumptions are common in individualist cultures, but not so in collectivist cultures where their introduction is likely to be met with resentment and resistance. Trompenaars's research findings indicate that the countries which are most individualistic in nature are Canada, the USA, the UK, Norway and Spain, while France, Greece, Kuwait and most Asian countries are best described as collectivist.

● *Neutral versus emotional*

This dimension is concerned with the ways in which individuals in certain cultures choose to express their emotions. Members of cultures which are neutral keep their feelings controlled and hidden, whereas members of cultures which are emotional show their feelings plainly. Not only does this have implications for communications between managers and employees from different national cultures generally, it is also likely to have a significant impact on the way that giving feedback is seen to be appropriate. Exhibiting emotion was found to be least acceptable in Japan, followed by Germany, Indonesia, the UK and Thailand and most acceptable in Italy, France and the USA.

● *Achievement versus ascription*

This dimension deals with how status and power in organisations are determined. In achievement-oriented cultures, employees are evaluated on how well they perform an allocated task or behaviour. Achieved status refers to 'doing'. In ascriptive cultures, status is attributed to particular types of people; for example older people, highly qualified employees and men. Ascribed status refers to 'being'. In ascriptive cultures, it is unlikely that management practices such as pay for performance will work well.

● *Sequential time versus synchronic time*

This dimension relates to whether people do things one after the other or several things at once. It involves differences between people's orientation to the past, present or future and between long and short time horizons. Trompenaars and Wooliams (1999: 33) argue that dilemmas can arise from being:

- more inclined toward step-by-step or parallel processing
- concerned with deadlines above quality, or placing quality first
- keen to win the race or shorten the course.

When considering the work of different authors on national culture it is important to remember that the unit of analysis is the nation-state and not the individual. The dimensions are, therefore, useful not for describing individuals, but for describing the social systems that those individuals are likely to have built. They are not in any way measures of individual personality.

Many multinational corporations (MNCs) have recognised the importance of being sensitive to the cultural context of host countries. However, the MNC's country of origin is a further cultural influence since research evidence suggests that this has a powerful effect on the top management of the company. In fact, while a host country's legal and institutional context may have a major effect on an MNC's HRM policies, this will not remove the home influence altogether. These questions can be explored further in Chapter 11, where an MNC forms the basis for the case study.

THE INTERNAL CONTEXT

Although the factors outlined above shape management approaches they still permit managers a degree of choice and the exercise of that choice will inevitably depend upon the company's management style and internal structure.

Management Style

One way of distinguishing between the approaches of different companies to human resource issues is to determine whether the organisation places an emphasis on developing relations with their employees as individuals (*individualism*), or whether they recognise that employees have a collective or group interest in the operation of the company (*collectivism*) (Figure 2.1).

Indeed, it is perfectly possible for managers to emphasise both dimensions simultaneously, and it is on this basis that a number of ideal types of management approach have been suggested. You should note that the terms 'individualism' and 'collectivism' are defined differently here from the way in which they were used by Trompenaars above.

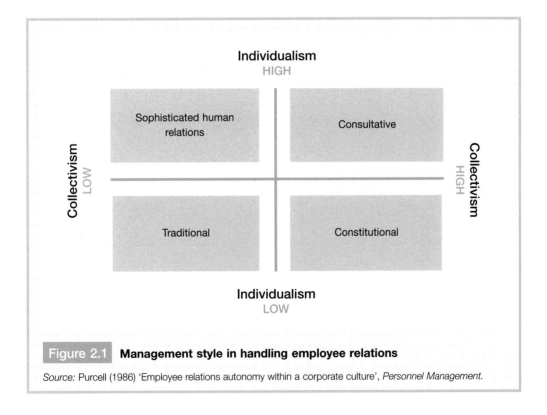

Figure 2.1 **Management style in handling employee relations**

Source: Purcell (1986) 'Employee relations autonomy within a corporate culture', *Personnel Management.*

- *Sophisticated human relations*

Employees (excluding short-term contract or subcontract labour) are viewed as the company's most valuable resource. Firms adopting this style often deliberately have above-average pay, clear internal labour market structures with promotion ladders, and periodic attitude surveys are used to harness employees' views. Emphasis is placed on flexible reward structures, employee appraisal systems linked to merit awards, internal grievance, and disciplinary and consultative procedures and there are extensive networks and methods of communication. The aim is to inculcate employee loyalty, commitment and dependency. As a by-product, many of these companies seek to make it unnecessary or unattractive for staff to unionise.

- *Consultative*

Similar to the sophisticated human relations companies, except that unions are recognised. The attempt is to build 'constructive' relationships with the unions and incorporate them into the organisational fabric. Wide-ranging discussions are held and extensive information provided to the unions on a whole range of decisions and plans, including aspects of strategic management; the 'right of last say', though, rests with management. Emphasis is also placed on techniques designed to enhance individual employee commitment to the firm and the need to accept change.

- *Traditional*

Labour is viewed as a factor of production and employee subordination is assumed to be part of the 'natural order' of the employment relationship. There is often a fear of outside union interference. Unionisation is opposed or unions are kept at arm's length.

- *Constitutional*

Somewhat similar to the traditionalists in basic value structures, especially for the unskilled and semi-skilled workers, but unions have been recognised for some time and are accepted as inevitable. Employee relations policies centre on the need for stability, control and the institutionalisation of conflict. Management prerogatives are defended through highly specific collective agreements, and careful attention is paid to the administration of agreements on the shop floor. The importance of management control is emphasised, with the aim of minimising or neutralising union constraints on both operational (line) and strategic (corporate) management. (Purcell, 1986: 39)

These are ideal types, but it is not difficult to think of examples of these categories. Several varieties of the sophisticated human relations type can be identified: Hewlett-Packard is a long-standing example. Many US companies which have opened plants in the UK have adopted this style. The consultative style of employee relations is most often found in other European countries, such as Germany where union recognition is common, and in Japan. Japanese companies are likely to deal with 'company unions' (that is unions which are not strictly independent from the organisation) but the approach is, nevertheless, still high on collectivism, since there is no requirement for employees to be represented by a trade union rather than other types of employee representatives. Some UK companies such as ICI would also fit this style. The best examples of the constitutional style are to be found in the USA, where it has been the predominant pattern in highly unionised companies since the New Deal legislation of the 1930s. However, this is also the style which typifies the management–union relationships of many large British companies. Examples of the traditional style might be franchises such as filling stations and some fast-food outlets.

Although this model has subsequently been refined (for example Purcell and Ahlstrand, 1994), its relative simplicity as an analytical tool makes it more attractive than the later management-style matrix (1994: 178) for present purposes.

You should bear in mind that companies often draw distinctions between different groups of employees within the company and adopt different management styles for each of these groups. For example, it is not uncommon for companies to adopt a sophisticated human relations style when managing managers, but a traditional style when managing non-managerial employees. Other companies will adopt a traditional style for temporary or part-time employees, while full-time or core staff are managed according to a consultative or sophisticated human relations style.

Despite the potential advantages of union recognition, many employers, especially in the USA and the UK, have become increasingly impatient with the constraints of having to manage employee relations through trade unions. In the political context of the 1980s and 90s, many sought to roll back the power of trade unions and to limit the scope and significance of collective bargaining, and this has led to an increasing emphasis on individualism rather than collectivism as the basis for employee relations.

However, the importance of political context must not be underestimated. The UK Labour government, for example, has recently introduced legislation (Employment Relations Act 1999) which enables trade unions to seek recognition from employers for the purposes of collective bargaining. The impact of this legislation remains to be seen, but is potentially far-reaching.

Internal Structure

While the structure of an organisation will not determine choices about human resources, research has shown that it can have a very strong influence on the way that human resources are managed (Purcell and Ahlstrand, 1994). Perhaps the organisational structure with the most direct impact on human resources is the multi-divisional or M-form, especially where the business is highly diversified. In the M-form company, each unit or division is relatively self-contained in that it has the resources to operate independently of other divisions. Each division is typically headed by an executive who is responsible for investment in facilities, capital and people as well as the division's development and performance. This structure is similar to dividing an organisation into several smaller companies, with the main difference being that each 'smaller' company is not itself completely independent.

M-form companies vary widely in their operating arrangements, but typically have a three-tiered structure: a corporate central office, divisions and operating plants or establishments. Three features of this structure are important for our purposes. First, the corporate head office is generally responsible for strategic planning, the development of guiding policies and courses of action, and the allocation of resources necessary for goal attainment. Second, profits are not automatically returned to the divisions which generated them, but are instead subject to a process of divisional bidding, with corporate management deciding on the allocation between competing demands in light of strategic need. Third, because of the high degree of diversification an extensive set of controls is established which seeks to regulate and monitor divisional behaviour. This includes regular financial audits or reporting requirements which provide comprehensive data on divisional performance and tie future funding to business success. Divisions which fail to meet financial targets often find themselves subject to reorganisation or fall victim to corporate intervention or divestment (Goold and Campbell, 1987).

This affects human resources in two ways. First, it becomes more likely that the corporate level will not see a need to develop integrated HRM policies across the organisation, since in a highly diversified business the message from the corporate office is 'provided you reach these targets we don't mind how you do it'. Second, because of the forces generated towards short-term financial reviews, it becomes harder at the operating unit level to develop and maintain long-run human resource policies. Although this is true for many M-form companies, not all of them rely on purely financial controls, particularly where the firm is a 'single-product' business which gives greater freedom to formulate and implement corporate-wide human resource policies (Purcell and Ahlstrand, 1994).

THE LINKS BETWEEN BUSINESS STRATEGY AND HRM STRATEGY

The debate about the link between HRM and business strategy is one of the most important to emerge in recent years. Some writers argue that in the past so-called 'personnel management' neglected strategic issues, favouring instead a more reactive stance aimed at securing employee relations stability (see Guest, 1987; Storey, 1992). While this view has been criticised for being stereotypical (Mabey and Salaman, 1995), it has helped to stimulate questioning about the relationship between HRM practices and strategic outcomes.

Three major perspectives on that relationship have been developed. The first, which can be termed 'HRM best practice', essentially argues that there is a specific set of HRM policies which are best practice and which lead to high levels of employee performance. This encompasses items such as teamwork, flexibility, quality and organisational commitment (Guest, 1987). Wood, for example, concludes a recent study with the claim: 'The implication of this research is that high commitment management is universally applicable' (1995: 57). Arguably this involves a particular approach to employee relations, emphasising unitary values and individualism, and challenging the role of unions.

A second approach, which has been termed the 'contingency' approach, argues that the choice of HRM strategy depends on the firm's business strategy. This involves ensuring a 'fit' between HRM strategy and business strategy. 'Internal fit' involves ensuring consistency between different HRM policies to ensure that they are self-reinforcing not conflicting. 'External fit' means ensuring that HRM strategy as a whole is compatible with and supports the business strategy of the firm. In this view, a cost-reduction business strategy, say, would imply a different set of HRM policies than a strategy based on innovation. An HRM strategy to fit with cost reduction might require deskilling, management control and downward pressure on wages. In contrast, one aimed at innovation would be likely to foster employee skills, autonomy and competitive wages.

The third approach to strategy which can be identified in the literature focuses on HRM's role in developing human and social capital. In this perspective, HRM makes its contribution to business strategy not so much by seeking a fit with the overall management approach as by shaping what have been termed the 'core competencies' (Prahalad and Hamel, 1990) of the organisation. These competencies are enhanced, it is argued, by the development of employee skills (human capital) and by increasing trustful interaction between employees (social capital). Human capital enhances productivity and innovation by extending the employees' behavioural repertoire, allowing a more flexible response to new technologies and work organisation. Social capital encourages more effective coordination and innovation through the sharing of knowledge via informal networks based on trust. Overall, the implication of this perspective is to highlight the long-term effects of HRM practices – on employee relations, culture and levels of trust – over their more formal characteristics.

These contrasting perspectives on HRM strategy are partly a reflection of different understandings of the way companies achieve high performance. In the first view, high performance comes from adopting a specific formula; put simply, high commitment leads to high performance. This can be criticised for not taking into account the influence of different market and organisational contexts – one size fits all is a questionable proposition (Mabey and Salaman, 1995). In the second view, management adapt their strategies rationally to ensure that their HRM policies fit with business strategy. While this recognises the importance of context, it possibly over-states management's ability to operate rationally, and, indeed, the extent to which HRM policies can be readily adapted to changing strategies. There is often a significant lag between change in business strategy and change in HRM practices. Reward systems, for example, are especially difficult to change. As Sparrow and Marchington note:

Organizations ... are experiencing high levels of rewards failure because most of their pay systems do not reflect strongly enough strategic thrusts towards quality, teamworking, and competition based on time. (1998: 13)

Chapter 4 provides an excellent example of some of the tensions that develop between organisational change and the established pay systems of an organisation.

In this light, the implications of the third approach may seem more attractive. It does not focus on fit, but recognises the long-term impact of HRM strategy in shaping the human and social capital of the organisation. By the same token, however, this approach underlines the limits of management's ability to shape these factors in the short term. There is also the argument that some elements of human and social capital are actually outside management's control.

Overall, these points should help us to understand that the link between HRM strategy and business strategy is a complex one, which repays viewing from a variety of perspectives. As a number of our cases, demonstrate, not only is the formulation of HRM strategy difficult to link to wider business strategy, but management's ability to implement desired changes is highly dependent on the history and context of the organisation. This will certainly test the closeness of the cooperation between senior management and HR specialists as we note below.

THE ROLE OF MANAGEMENT IN HR

Having largely relinquished the welfare role that characterised its early years, the HRM profession is now moving away from acting as a go-between in employee relations to become a more fully integrated part of management structure. This means that HRM is increasingly a shared task and, as with most shared tasks, there can be tensions between those people who share the tasks. Traditionally the HRM influence on line management was viewed in terms of a staff–line distinction. The HRM function was seen as a staff grouping which supported line managers through the 'dotted line' influence of advice and constraint. Research now suggests a very different role for HRM (for example Sparrow and Marchington, 1998), with greater emphasis being placed on mediating and facilitating line management's control of HRM tasks, greater focus on quality issues and organisational development and an ever-increasing need to justify the cost of HRM activities.

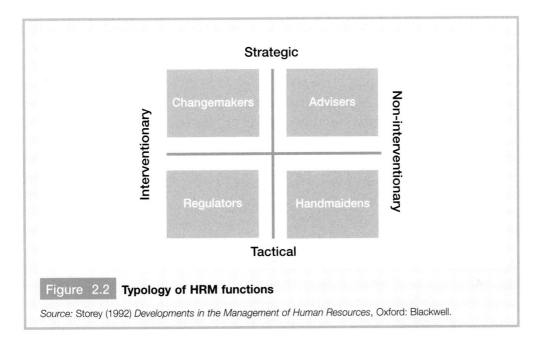

Figure 2.2 **Typology of HRM functions**

Source: Storey (1992) *Developments in the Management of Human Resources*, Oxford: Blackwell.

The move away from bureaucratic organisation structures and the adoption of HRM perspectives by senior managers suggest that the line–staff distinction is a poor way of understanding the current relationship, especially given recent trends towards the devolution of more HRM tasks to line managers. Whether this devolution leads to the diffusion or neglect of good HRM practices probably depends on the kind of relationship which emerges between line managers and the HRM function. This relationship may vary from organisation to organisation, according to two factors: the degree of discretion afforded to the HRM function and the level of intervention by HRM practitioners (Figure 2.2). In each of the cases that follow you will be asked to analyse the nature and role of the HRM function and how this has affected choices about HRM and the ease with which new initiatives are implemented. The quotations which accompany Storey's definitions give some idea of how these models work in practice.

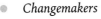 *Changemakers*

These seek to put employee relations on a new footing, one

which emphasises the needs of the business. This may be done either from a distinctive human resource perspective, or as a fully integrated member of the top management team. These distinctions are reflected in the following quotes:

*C*hris has brought a breath of fresh air to the board. Our 'analysis' of people management issues was clouded by our obsession with relative remuneration packages and the like. We now have a much wider vista; talk of retention, development and career planning has become more meaningful and serious. Oddly, our people-management policies now also seem to make far more business sense. The Board feels more in control of the massive culture change which we are undoubtedly undergoing. (Storey: 182–3)

*W*e always have to remember that we are in business to make money. That is really what it's all about in the end. My portfolio on the Board normally takes in personnel and corporate affairs. But, to be perfectly honest, I don't regard myself as a personnel specialist anymore. (Storey: 186)

● *Advisers*
Advisers act as internal consultants, and are in tune with recent developments. They allow line and general management to make the running on HRM initiatives.

I try to ensure that discussions are between line managers and their opposite numbers on the trade union side. Me and my people are not to be seen as go-betweens or, still less, as people who make the line roll-over. The line managers have to make the commitment to the solution. I like to see them getting on with it and I like to keep out of their hair. (Storey: 170)

- *Regulators*

  The HRM function in this category formulates employment rules – personnel procedures and union agreements and so on – and then monitors their observance.

  *I*t is only a few years ago that the production managers here would pass all their IR problems on to us. More than once I have come into this very room (a conference room) to find a plant manager facing a group of stewards whose lads had already walked off the job. As soon as I came through the door the so-called manager would stand up and say, 'Ah I'm glad you've arrived to sort this out' and then he'd head off out! (Storey: 176)

- *Handmaidens*

  These are specialists who operate in a reactive mode, with an almost submissive relationship to their client.

  *W*e had a meeting last week with the new subsector managers. We set out our stall and we said to them 'Look here's what we do, now, what do you want to sign off for?' (Storey: 172)

It is clear from Storey's work that there is no one best way for the HRM function to be managed. Moreover, these roles are not fixed over time; changes can and do occur in organisational expectations of the HRM function. Also, HRM specialists have jobs at different levels of the organisation, which means that it is possible for different people within the function to have different roles. For example, at Ford of Europe the employee affairs directorate has tended to play a 'changemaker' role, while at plant level the personnel manager plays an adviser role.

$\mathcal{P}$ATTERNS OF EMPLOYMENT

One of the changes which is setting a new agenda for HRM is a move away from managing the contract of employment and towards the contract for performance. One is focused on the job and job-related pay, and the other on the individual and performance-related pay. This trend towards individualism in employee relations is often complemented by human resource systems designed to regulate performance. The emphasis is not on particular jobs or roles, but on the individual's ability to respond flexibly to changing objectives. In the face of moves away from bureaucratic hierarchies and towards flatter, more market facing structures, many companies are redefining the individual's contribution. This involves a move towards a more flexible clustering of individual competencies and achievements. For employees the implications are double-edged. Unlike the security offered by role-based status, individual performance is highly variable and open to comparison with that of peers. Chapters 3 and 4 look at some of the problems associated with contracts for performance, the difficulties of adapting this to a teamworking environment and the links between performance and reward.

In other ways employment is also becoming more insecure. Instead of a full-time job, more flexible working arrangements are now common, such as annual hours, part-time working and temporary contracts, and the notion of 'employability' is rapidly gaining ground over the traditional 'job-for-life'. Chapter 9 deals directly with issues relating to the impact of job insecurity on employees who survive redundancy. It explores what organisations can do to ameliorate the impact, and looks at the reasons which will determine whether or not companies do in fact act in this way.

While many organisations have identified the advantages of a performance-oriented approach, most have only adopted it in a piecemeal fashion. This suggests that many firms are failing to integrate their various HRM activities. In terms of the HRM strategy described above, this can be viewed as a lack of *internal fit*. Without good internal fit, organisations, while emphasising individual performance, may be failing to ensure that individuals' goals are actually contributing to overall performance. This is a crucial aspect of good HRM, and one that is all too often overlooked.

THE GAP BETWEEN POLICY AND PRACTICE

Traditionally, much HRM work has been about developing policies to do with recruitment, selection, promotion, appraisal and so on. Policies are statements of principle, intended to be informed by strategy and to guide practice. They can clarify situations, reduce dependence on individuals, produce consistent behaviour and help employees and managers to know where they stand. In addition, they often form the organisational response to external pressures; when a new piece of legislation appears on the statute book, managers wait for policy guidance on its influence.

However, from experience we know that there is often a gap between an organisation's stated policy and its actual practice. Why is this? Whether or not a particular policy is implemented in practice is affected by a variety of factors. For example, it is affected by the appropriateness of the policy, by different priorities of line or HR managers, or different understandings of what the policy was meant to achieve, as well as possible conflicts between policies. In addition, the process through which the policy was developed is vitally important to its acceptance, and winning consent to particular policies will probably require the involvement of concerned parties in this process.

Finally, a problem common to HRM functions is the failure to evaluate or monitor policies. Unless policies are monitored and evaluated against concrete objectives, no one will know whether or not objectives are being met, or whether a gap between policy and practice actually exists.

CONCLUSION

This chapter has highlighted the contextual nature of management practice, and the problems of following general recipes for success. In doing so it has tended to cast doubt on the 'Holy Grail' of HRM, that is, the links between business strategy and HRM strategy. This is not to suggest that a strategic approach to HRM is impossible, but that it requires more than a few policy changes to bring about an effective fit that will actually enhance business performance. Although the rational adaptation of practice to strategic objectives is an alluring goal, it is easily frustrated in the HRM area by a range of factors over which management have no control, and sometimes more by factors over which they do have control, that is, patterns of work organisation, flexibility and employment conditions. This tension within managerial objectives, as well as the impact of context, helps to explain the chronic gap that exists between rhetoric and reality in HRM practice. While HRM strategies are expressed in the rational language of means and ends, the intractable problems of conflicting pressures, employee resistance and external pressures tend to drive a wedge between policy and outcomes.

In short, a point to bear in mind in reviewing subsequent chapters is that HRM policies are constantly afflicted by unintended consequences. And this observation not only applies to our case studies themselves, but could be equally applied to the recommendations which students will derive from their analysis of those cases. Understanding how organisations deal with these unintended and unanticipated factors is a major clue to understanding how HRM can succeed (or fail) to be a strategic issue within management. Companies where HRM specialists spend the greater part of their time fire fighting and dealing with the failure of previous policies risk being locked into a vicious circle. If HRM is seen as inherently messy and unsatisfactory – something managers just have to cope with – it will be downgraded and devalued in management's eyes. Its strategic dimensions will never be fully recognised. On the other hand, where management are able to lift their eyes from the present messiness, and focus on the wider horizon of the long-term benefits achievable through HRM, a more promising scenario can be envisaged.

REFERENCES

Employment Gazette (1992) 'Employment statistics', Historical supplement No. 3, **100**(6): 1–59.

Goold, M. and Campbell, A. (1987) *Strategies and Styles: The Role of the Centre in Managing Diversified Corporations*. Oxford: Blackwell.

Guest, D. (1987) 'Human resource management: its implications for industrial relations', *Journal of Management Studies*, **24**(5): 503–21.

Hofstede, G. (1984) *Culture's Consequences: International Differences in Work-related Values*. Beverley Hills, CA: Sage.

Hutchinson, S., Kinnie, N., Purcell, J., Collinson, M., Scarbrough, H. and Terry, M. (1998) 'Getting Fit, Staying Fit: Developing Lean and Responsive Organizations', *Issues in People Management*, **15**.

Mabey, C. and Salaman, G. (1995) *Human Resource Strategies*. Oxford: Blackwell.

Marginson, P. and Sisson, K. (1994) 'The structure of transnational capital in Europe: the emerging Euro-company and its implications for industrial relations' in Hyman, R. and Ferner, A. (eds) *New Frontiers in European Industrial Relations*. Oxford: Basil Blackwell.

Prahalad, C.K. and Hamel, G. (1990) 'The core competencies of the corporation', *Harvard Business Review*, May–June, pp. 79–91.

Purcell, J. (1986) 'Employee relations autonomy within a corporate culture', *Personnel Management*, February, pp. 38–40.

Purcell, J. and Ahlstrand, B. (1994) *Human Resource Management in the Multi-divisional Company*. Oxford: Oxford University Press.

Scarbrough, H., Swan, J. and Preston, J. (1998) *Knowledge Management and the Learning Organization: A Review of the Literature*. London: Institute of Personnel and Development.

Sparrow, P. and Marchington, M. (eds) (1998) *Human Resource Management: The New Agenda*. Harlow: Prentice Hall.

Storey, J. (1992) *Developments in the Management of Human Resources*. Oxford: Blackwell.

Trompenaars, F. (1993) *Riding The Waves of Culture: Understanding Cultural Diversity in Business*. London: Nicholas Brearly.

Trompenaars, F. and Wooliams, P. (1999) 'First class accommodation', *People Management*, April, pp. 30–7.

Wood, S. (1995) 'The four pillars of HRM: are they connected?' *Human Resource Management Journal*, **5**(5): 48–58.

CHAPTER THREE

ALCAN:

MANAGING CHANGE

THE CASE OF TEAMWORK

PAUL EDWARDS AND MARTYN WRIGHT

IN THIS CASE STUDY WE AIM TO:

- EXAMINE the spread of teamworking within organisations

- CONSIDER the factors affecting the success of teamworking initiatives

- ANALYSE the experience of one organisation in developing teamworking to address business problems.

This case is based on the introduction and operation of an advanced team system at an aluminium smelter owned by the Canadian multi-national, Alcan, and located at Lynemouth, Northumberland. The story runs from 1991 to 1998. An important point about learning from the case concerns the conditions which underlay the successful implementation of teamworking here. It is not a case of 'how to introduce teamworking' in general but of how teams operated in a particular context.

DEBATES ON TEAMWORKING

The idea of working in teams rather than as isolated individuals may seem to be so obvious as to require no comment. Many jobs, as varied as dockers unloading ships and medical staff performing operations, have always been organised on team principles. It is also notable that for many years workers complained that they should be given more discretion and that teamwork, as it emerged in the 1980s, had many forebears such as Quality of Working Life experiments in the 1960s. If teams are so natural and so in tune with workers' preferences, why are firms reluctant to introduce them? We return to this question having indicated the main variants of teamwork and evidence on its extent.

Teamworking is one of the most popular new forms of human resource management. Surveys frequently claim that as many as 40% of organisations in the UK and other countries use self-managed teams. One of the reasons for this widespread adoption is that teamworking is central to production systems such as 'lean production' and the 'sociotechnical systems model'. It is important to note, however, that the role of teamworking may be very different according to the requirements of each system. For example, we can distinguish between the requirements of sociotechnical systems (STSs) and lean production (LP). Table 3.1 is a summary of their main features.

The STS model is based on Swedish practice, notably experiments by Volvo at its Kalmar and Uddevalla plants (Berggren, 1994).

Table 3.1 Contrasting models of team organisation

	Lean production	Sociotechnical systems
Task range	Simple	Complex
Quality:		
Process improvement	Through SPC, TQM,	Informal
Employee involvement	QCs, suggestion schemes	Informal
Skills	Learnt by on-the-job training	Broad
Discipline	Group and management	Group
Group work:		
Membership	Mandatory	Voluntary
Election of leader	Management	Group
Autonomy	Low	High
Market:		
Character	Mass	Niche
Volume	High	Low

Sources: Adapted from Appelbaum and Batt (1994: 44–9); Fröhlich and Pekruhl (1996: 86); Hutchinson et al. (1998: 25–6).

The essence of the model is a team of workers with long cycle times and the discretion to allocate work tasks between team members. Teams also elect their own leaders and exercise judgement about quality issues. In its most developed form at Uddevalla, teams assembled whole cars. The model is often seen as appropriate only to specialist niche markets where production is low volume and high value added. This contrasts with the LP model which was originally developed by Toyota in Japan. The key points about LP are that the task range remains quite simple, quality is handled through precise procedures which give workers little discretion and worker autonomy in teams is tightly restricted.

It follows from this analysis that 'teams' come in many forms, but the more advanced forms of teamworking remain rare (Geary, 1995). By 'advanced', we mean systems which embrace:

- teams that are given significant autonomy over the allocation of work tasks

- the limitation or removal of direct supervision

- systematic means to allow teams to discuss work organisation, such as problem-solving groups or regular team briefings.

These innovations will often be accompanied by wider changes in communication systems and by 'single status' for manual and white-collar staff.

*H*OW WIDESPREAD IS TEAMWORK?

Some survey evidence suggests that teamwork is widespread. Osterman (1994) reports a survey in the US which suggested that 55% of establishments used self-directed teams; moreover, 41% of all establishments claimed that this system was not just a marginal experiment but covered at least half the workforce. Definitions are often imprecise, however, and it is important to establish the depth of teamworking. A survey across ten European countries was the first to do this systematically (European Foundation, 1997). It began by offering a definition of teamworking (or 'group delegation') as a situation where 'rights and responsibilities are granted to groups of employees to carry out their common tasks without constant reference back to management'. On this definition, 33% of establishments claimed to practice group work, and only 17% had it for at least half their workers. The study went on to measure *scope* (the range of issues on which work groups have an influence including the choice of team leader and allocation of work tasks) and *autonomy* (the degree of independence enjoyed by teams). These were combined to give a measure of 'intensity', which gives an overall measure of how much influence work groups enjoy. Using this more stringent definition of teams, the study found extensive teamworking to be rare. Only 5% of establishments had high scores on intensity. Where group work existed at all, it fell between the STS and LP patterns, 'with a tendency towards the latter' (European Foundation, 1997: 59). In short, the practice of teamwork may fall far short of the rhetoric.

FACTORS WHICH PROMOTE TEAMWORK

Case study evidence points to the conditions which promote team-working. The first is *technology*. Continuous process operations encourage teamwork because there is a natural tendency for work to be organised around crews rather than individual operations. A series of studies suggests that teamworking often fails to become established for relatively low-skilled work in assembly conditions. For example, Pollert (1996) reports on a teamwork experiment in a chocolate factory and concludes that it had failed, with the ideology of cooperation contradicting the reality of fragmented and tightly controlled work. STSs are most likely where production runs are short and products are complex and involve high added value. LP is seen as more appropriate to mass production.

A second condition, the *existing culture of work group relationships*, has been less debated. In cases such as those analysed by Pollert, assembly lines predominate and there is no basis for any sense of work group cohesion. Other technologies can promote cohesion and group identity, which can in turn contribute to acceptance of team-working. Where workers are long-serving and where they have a strong sense of group identity, they may be more willing to accept the idea of teams than where they are fragmented.

Related to the second issue is a third, *the role of trade unions*. Many of the more famous team experiments in the US, such as those at the Saturn Corporation, operate in unionised environments. Survey evidence in the US and the UK shows that relatively advanced forms of human resource management, including team-work, are more common in union than non-union settings. Yet evidence also shows that it is common for organisations to introduce teams alongside efforts to reduce the role of unions. In these circumstances there is the problem of 'mixed messages', and work-force commitment to teamwork can be lost. It is not the case that unions are necessary for teamworking, but where they are well established they may make a positive contribution. Minimising their role may have the negative effect of undermining acceptance of teams.

A fourth issue is the role of a *triggering event*. At the Digital plant at Ayr, Scotland, a more advanced form of teamwork developed on the back of a threat to the plant's existence. Teams operated without supervisors and were responsible for a range of tasks (Buchanan and McCalman, 1989). Generally favourable employee responses and business performance outcomes were produced, but, as Storey and Sisson (1993: 94) note, this may have resulted from the fact that the study was conducted soon after the change programme, so that initial optimism had not had time to dissipate.

A fifth issue concerns the *national and company environment*. Sweden is the home of the STS model, which reflects conditions in that country, notably the very strong position of trade unions and established ideas of management–union partnership. It is thus important that Volvo has not used the STS model in its plants in other countries. Environments such as the UK are generally seen as relatively hostile to teamwork because the trade union role is different and because managements are typically less in favour of ideas of worker autonomy.

Finally, whether or not teamworking is introduced will often turn on the *benefits for management* and this leads us to ask why teams are used so rarely when they appear to have evident benefits. Appelbaum and Berg (1996) offer some answers to this question. First, benefits tend to be long term, since it takes time for teams to be implemented. Many firms are driven by short-term financial pressures. Related to this are issues to do with corporate control: if benefits are long term, but firms are subject to immediate takeover threats, investment in innovative HR practices will be restricted. Work reorganisation entails short-run costs, which reduce profitability and raise the takeover threat, while the long-term gains may be reaped by the predator and not the originator. Second, investing is more likely in some sectors than others. Some industries, such as pharmaceuticals, need to innovate to retain competitive advantage, and here one may expect to see a long-term approach. In such cases, there is little alternative to investment. Other factors commonly identified include the fear by managers that teams will undermine their own authority. Institutional and contextual forces thus shape the ease with which teams are introduced, and the likelihood of their survival.

THE CASE STUDY

The Lynemouth Smelter in 1990

The evidence is derived from research at the plant in 1995 and 1997. The first study covered interviews with all levels of employee and a questionnaire survey of shop-floor workers. In 1997, we revisited the plant and interviewed many of our key informants again.

Aluminium is a long-term, capital-intensive business. Some of Alcan's Canadian smelters were built in the 1940s and were still in production in the 1990s. Lynemouth began production in 1972. Its basic operating design was established when the plant was built and this is largely fixed. There are three plants on site. The *carbon plant* manufactures anodes by mixing and baking carbon to form large blocks. These are taken to the *pot rooms* where they are placed in large crucibles ('pots'). In these an electric current is passed through alumina to produce molten aluminium. This is then tapped and taken to the *casting plant* where it is cast into ingots. A major cost of production is energy. Lynemouth is coal fired, and its costs are thus greater than its counterparts in Alcan's main base of Quebec, where there is abundant hydroelectric power. Smelting is a continuous process, operating 24 hours per day, all year round. From its inception the plant ran on a system of 12-hour shifts. Workers divide their time between working 'on-line' servicing the pots, and rest periods spent off-line in the rest room. These rest breaks may take up several hours in any one shift.

In 1990, the plant employed 780 employees. Many workers had been with the plant since it opened. All shop-floor and craft workers were male, a few women were employed in clerical posts. Wages were good in relation to those of the locality, where unemployment was high and many jobs in manufacturing and heavy industry were lost during the 1980s. Labour turnover was therefore low. Work organisation was fairly conventional, with each group of workers being responsible to a supervisor who dealt with all day-to-day production matters such as the allocation of tasks, granting of holidays and shift rotas. Supervisors worked the same shifts as their work crews. The majority of workers were production operatives and craft workers, virtually all of whom belonged to trade unions. Production workers belonged to the GMB union which was numerically predominant and which had a full-time 'convenor' (a senior shop steward, elected by the stewards' committee but paid by management). Unions were also recognised by management in respect of white-collar staff,

although membership levels were lower and influence was weaker.

The climate of industrial relations could be characterised as suspicious and mistrustful but not openly antagonistic. On the positive side, the plant appears to have had few serious strikes.

Among craft workers, multiskilling was established from 1972 so that, apart from a basic division between electrical and mechanical trades, there were no notable demarcations between different trades. This feature distinguished the plant from many manufacturing sites in the UK at the time. On the negative side, there was a wide-

---

Table 3.2 Industrial relations in 1986

Terms of reference: to review communications and the climate of industrial relations, and to make recommendations.

Analysis:

Many plants have worse communications and industrial relations. Positive features include 'a willingness of people anywhere to get stuck in when an emergency arises'. The single status agreement introduced when the plant opened continues to be 'well in advance of many companies'.

Problems centre on a lack of real trust, so that both sides use existing agreements to seek their own immediate ends. There is a sense of distance and an unwillingness to establish shared ownership of issues. Many matters go through committees but there is insufficient action and progress tends to be slow.

Illustrative quotes from shop-floor employees identified complaints as lack of consultation, including the making of technical changes which would have been better if based on the input of staff on the ground; and a sense of distance from management.

Recommendations:

1.	Implement team briefing to allow focused discussion between work groups and supervisors.
2.	Consider departmental and plant consultative committees.
3.	Review industrial relations with unions, including establishing the role of unions as not being to veto change but to 'represent their members to management – not management to members'.

Source: Musgrave (1998) 'British Alcan Lynemouth: Review of Industrial Relations'.

spread perception that it was hard to implement change and that communication was poor. This picture can be amplified by reference to Table 3.2, which is a summary of the conclusions of a study carried out in 1986, at the request of management and all the unions, by Peter Musgrave of the Industrial Society.

The underlying message was that management wanted to impose change by insisting on the application of parts of existing agreements, rather than involving the unions. For their part the unions saw negotiations in the light of their own sectional interests and employees reported a lack of consultation by management. This contributed to a growing sense of worker dissatisfaction, which was adversely affecting the quality of production. The report recommended the use of consultative committees and team briefing, and that management develop more cooperative relations with trade unions. There was, however, little action on the report's recommendations.

Increasing Competition in the Aluminium Industry

The world price of aluminium began to fall from an all-time high of US$2,705 a tonne in 1988 and reached its lowest level, of $1,055 a tonne, in 1993. At the same time, there was growing overcapacity with the emergence of new producers such as Venezuela and declining demand. Alcan's worldwide output remained more or less static between 1988 and 1993 while employment fell from 56,000 to 46,000. The firm made losses during the years 1991–93.

In 1991 came a critical event, the closure of one of Lynemouth's two pot lines together with the redundancy of about half the workforce. The decision to reduce capacity was made at Alcan head office in Canada and the plant had little influence over the decision. It was plant managers' responsibility to carry through the redundancies, which they did with great speed. There was little consultation about the process. Workers were chosen for redundancy according to their records of capability.

Options for Change

As a high-cost producer with only a single line in operation in 1991, Lynemouth's future was clearly in doubt. Management were under intense pressure to raise the level of production efficiency. They had to do so rapidly, and without spending large sums on capital investment. Several options were open to managers in the wake of the redundancies:

(a) One possibility was to act decisively to reduce the role of trade unions or even to remove their bargaining rights altogether. This approach was growing in popularity at the time and it was followed by several large firms. Several managers felt that union intransigence was a key barrier to improvement. Undermining union influence would strengthen the position of supervisors, by enabling them to apply punitive measures against uncooperative workers. Ultimately, this might help to reassert management control of the shop floor. An increase in work effort might have been expected as a result of the 'fear factor' and the plant's performance measures might have been expected to improve. The downside to such a proposal was the risk of disruption by a strong and well-organised union body. Any prolonged stoppage might have serious effects. There was a risk of damage to the pots if they were allowed to cool, while restarting the process once it had stopped would be a complex operation which might take several months.

(b) A second option would be to establish more cooperative relations with trade unions, based on existing patterns of negotiation. Management could consult more meaningfully with union representatives, and attempt to agree rather than impose work changes. This approach had the advantage of minimising any possibility of disruption but might also have delayed the implementation of reforms. The 1990 collective agreement, for example, took nine months to negotiate. A large number of parties were required to agree before any settlement could be reached, as the plant recognised numerous craft, manual and non-manual unions, and bargained separately with each of them.

(c) The third option was to win employee consent by reforming the communications system and by promoting employee involvement. This has been a favoured strategy of several British firms, which do not directly attack union rights but confine them to the specifics of wage bargaining. Change in work organisation is then pursued without bargaining. The spirit of Musgrave's reforms, including introducing team briefing and consultative committees, might be adopted. Measures to improve employee job satisfaction might also be considered, including teams. The risks in these changes were that the plant's unions would refuse to cooperate, or even undermine the initiatives. Such fundamental changes as teams might also destabilise the plant at a time when it was most vulnerable and would also take a long time to implement.

The new personnel manager, appointed in 1990, was known to have had experience of teamwork in previous plants. It was also rumoured that he had been brought in to promote similar approaches at Lynemouth. Thus it was possible that more senior managers in the UK favoured a 'new approach'. Alcan plants in other countries were also known to be experimenting with teamwork. However, it was not in the firm's tradition to instruct local managers in the

HR field, and it is unlikely that there was any standard blueprint that the plant could use, still less an expectation that it must follow any central instruction. Thus, it was for local managers to make their choices.

Teamworking, 1991–95

In the event, developments followed a path outlined under options (b) and (c) above. Teamworking was introduced with the explicit cooperation of plant trade unions. Key milestones are summarised in Table 3.3. Reforms were implemented in a number of stages.

In 1991, teamworking was introduced. This encompassed team briefing, job rotation and a degree of multiskilling. The key event came in 1994, with the end of direct supervision. In place of supervisors, team leaders were appointed by management from existing team members following a formal application procedure. The team leader was made responsible for team briefing and the coordination and scheduling of work. However, he had no authority over discipline. He received an additional weekly allowance of £18, which compared with the average annual pay (including shift allowance) of team members of £18,000 (that is, the pay supplement over team members was about 5%). In addition, 'accredited instructors' were responsible for evaluating training needs and scheduling and carrying out training of other team members. Their allowance was £9 per week.

Direct supervision in production areas was abolished and supervisors in these spheres were made redundant. Teams became semi-autonomous. Supervisors were

Table 3.3	Work restructuring at Lynemouth 1990–95
1990	New management team appointed at the plant, including incoming works director and personnel manager.
1991	Closure of Line 1; approximately half of the workforce was made redundant. Teamwork was formally introduced, including elements of team briefing, job rotation and off-line project work.
1992–93	Hierarchy with a large number of jobs and grades replaced by a flatter structure with nine grades covering all except senior management. Staff terms, including salaried status and sickness leave, extended to production workers. Single table collective bargaining introduced.
1994	Supervisory staff in production areas, numbering approximately fifty, are removed. 'Team leader' and 'accredited instructor' positions created. Nine 'group leader' positions are created, which carry the formal disciplinary powers of first line management. Appointees are previous supervisors and other middle managers. Two-year pay settlement negotiated.

not taken out of craft areas, such as maintenance and the garage. These sectors accounted for the 18 supervisors, from an original 49, that remained in place. Teams were given some responsibility for monitoring output, quality, aspects of safety and, in certain cases, budgeting. Nine 'group leader' (GL) positions were created. GLs were intended to have a facilitating and problem-solving role, albeit with the disciplinary powers of first line management held in reserve. Their function, ostensibly, was not to 'oversee' production and they were not attached to particular shifts.

Introducing Teamwork

In relation to the process by which these changes were made, two themes stand out. First, there was initial scepticism on the part of some production managers, who felt that workers could not be trusted to work without direct supervision. According to the personnel manager, they were slowly won over by evidence that teams could produce efficiently. He had made a point of checking output figures when teams were first introduced, so as to be able to demonstrate the benefits to production managers. By 1995, the senior management team accepted teamwork principles. In the view of the new plant manager, recently appointed from Canada, there was no real alternative to teams.

Second, teamwork was introduced through discussion with the unions, and it encouraged further developments in indus-

trial relations. Some training courses were held, symbolically, in union training centres, and union leaders in the plant were involved in detailed discussions about the process. It was generally agreed that, since 1991, a marked change in the climate of industrial relations had taken place. Collective industrial action was absent. Pay negotiations were now much more speedily resolved and there was 'single table bargaining' (that is, encompassing all the unions in one bargaining session, replacing the previous separate negotiations). GMB stewards stated that industrial relations had 'changed dramatically' since 1991. Now, relations between unions and management were 'more stable', and there was 'more discussion'. There was general agreement that shop stewards had not sought to undermine the authority of GLs, and no conflict over the role of shop stewards and GLs had surfaced. However, GLs felt that stewards were reluctant to negotiate for them, especially over work loads and additional payment.

Did Teamworking Work?

Did teamworking work, that is, did it produce results in terms of staff satisfaction, effectiveness of work organisation and productivity? Research in 1995 suggested that it did. On satisfaction and commitment, interviews and questionnaire returns indicated a greater sense of autonomy and participation among shop-floor workers.

This did not mean, however, that there was a complete sharing of views with management. Workers were clear that the divide between manager and worker was as sharp as ever and that the enforcement of discipline was not part of the teams' duties. This approach was different from some teamwork experiments, where teams have developed self-discipline. The difference reflected the workers' solidarity and independent traditions. There was thus a pragmatic acceptance of teams, which did not translate into wider trust in management.

On work organisation, there were increases in multiskilling, and there were clear examples of improved flexibility. For example, team members would work a crane as required, rather than wait for a dedicated crane driver. Yet such developments remained within clear limits. The fundamental technical layout of the plant was unaltered, and workers continued to rely on technical staff for the monitoring of the production process. Producing aluminium calls for a close control of the chemical processes involved, and each plant had specialist staff who kept the plant within its operating parameters. Technical expertise was often highly specialised, for example anodes were baked in furnaces, and there was a special technology for lining the furnaces with bricks. Shop-floor workers lacked serious engagement with the details of the technology.

In relation to productivity, a series of performance data going back to 1972 included several indicators showing improvement throughout this period. It was hard to assess the effects of teamwork, given the relatively short period for which it was in operation, but it showed no dramatic improvement over previous experience. Thus it is not the case that teamwork promoted an upsurge in productivity from a static situation. But it is also arguable that teamwork contributed to productivity. First, the former work organisation may have been running up to its limits of technical efficiency. Teamwork offered new forms of flexibility. Second, teamwork was part of a wider change of atmosphere. It helped to promote a sense of confidence and direction. Although it is impossible to be sure, it may be that without innovation in work organisation the plant might not have survived and have attracted investment for the reopening of Line 1, to which we now turn.

Teamworking, 1996–98

Despite the improvement in work relations and process efficiency between 1991 and 1995, Lynemouth, as a small, relatively high-cost producer, remained vulnerable to closure. This changed in 1996, with the announcement that Line 1 was to reopen. An investment of £80m in new equipment would double the production capacity of the plant, and require a major programme of recruitment. Plant management were faced with a new dilemma. Teams gained acceptance during a period of employee fears about job security. This pressure was now lifted. Management became concerned that teams might become complacent and that the unions might start to harden their bargaining stance.

Three major reforms were introduced between 1996 and 1998:

- Teams were given greater autonomy. The number of group leaders was reduced from nine to five, and they were confined to the day shift. There is now no management presence on site at nights or weekends. The role of group leader appeared to be increasingly uncertain since it entailed neither supervision of a particular part of the plant nor any specific functional responsibility.

- The unions were asked to recommend the number of new hires, based on their estimates of staffing requirements in each area of the expanded plant. A figure of 154 additional recruits was agreed, which was very close to managers' estimates.

- Responsibility for hiring new staff, and for assessing applications for internal transfers, was devolved to shop-floor workers. For the 154 jobs available, there were 1,200 applications, of which 700 were supported by existing staff and 500 were unsolicited. Applicants for jobs were interviewed by panels each comprising three shop-floor workers, one from each section of the plant. Each

panel had the absolute right to make decisions as to whom to hire, and any one member had the power of veto.

Dissatisfaction with Teamwork

By late 1997, the overall picture of teamwork from a shop-floor point of view was favourable. Senior managers and workers felt that significant change had been made. However, for middle managers and technical staff, the view was very different. In 1995, these groups had expressed some reservations about teams. Two years later, their doubts had hardened into feelings of frustration and resentment. Overall, white-collar staff felt undervalued and increasingly marginalised from decision-making. Morale had plummeted. The comments of a maintenance engineer in 1997 illustrate the point. The position of middle ranking staff, he says, deteriorated sharply in the past two years. Management, he claimed, 'treat us like shit'. He recounted one instance of a senior manager greeting IT staff with 'good morning, overheads'. He used to work a lot of additional hours but now worked strictly to his contract hours of 8 a.m.–4.30 p.m., even taking his fifteen minutes 'bathing time' to shower at the end of the shift. Other employees were also said to be confining their efforts to their standard hours. Many technical and other middle grade staff, it was reported, were seeking and would readily accept employment with other companies. Others said they would eagerly take early retirement, if offered.

Group leaders, particularly, felt that their status and authority were being eroded. Teams had taken on many of the tasks traditionally performed by the group leaders. The latter had taken on more mundane duties, such as calculating daily output figures, a job formerly done by a staff clerk. One group leader expressed his resentment at these changes. Another said he was disillusioned and that his colleagues had simply 'switched off'. This sense of dissatisfaction permeated the cadre of graduate entrants. One said that the work he was being given to do was not sufficiently demanding. The appraisal system was inadequate for discussing these issues, he said, because management refused to listen.

Teamwork was part of the reason why technical staff felt that their status had diminished, and that their job territory was under threat. One engineer noted that maintenance now had to respond to the wishes of production staff, often in ways that were not helpful. For example, teams now felt that the crane, which had been in operation for 25 years, ran too fast and the engineer had to make costly alterations to it. Pay was also a source of grievance for white-collar workers. Management, they felt, believed that non-manuals were overpaid. Many non-manuals had been taken off shift work, and had lost their shift allowance, which might be as much as £5,000 per annum for some workers. This also affected their pension entitlements which, in a plant with an ageing workforce, bred uncertainty. One engineer complained that his contractual allowance of £30 per month for overseeing shift staff had simply been removed, without consultation. Another bemoaned the £700 annual standby allowance which was awarded to some technical staff but, inexplicably, not to others.

Staff claimed that management were aware of their grievances but refused to address them. Teamwork, it was argued, was driven by senior management. Middle management dared not confront the production teams: 'it is now the rule not to blame the production teams, who are untouchable', as one engineer put it. According to one respondent, production operatives could perfectly well operate some equipment but management tolerated their refusal to do so.

These discontents were important in themselves. They also pointed to some possible further issues. Some managers felt that there was an atmosphere of complacency, with shop-floor workers feeling that they should not exert themselves unduly and with earlier practices such as leaving before the end of a shift creeping back in. It was not easy to establish how common such practices were, and they may well have remained marginal and unusual. But they indicated two issues: the possibility of complacency creeping in now that the future of the plant was secure, and the challenge of developing teamwork further.

CASE ANALYSIS – THE ISSUES

In analysing this case study you should address the following questions:

1. How would you describe Alcan's management style? How would you describe the role and status of the HR function in Alcan? How did these factors affect the company's decisions in relation to teamworking?

2. What were the main conditions encouraging the choice of teamwork in 1990 rather than one of the other possible options? Was this a good choice in light of their business strategy and competitive position? How typical do you think that Lynemouth was of management approaches in the UK?

3. Why do you think that it took until 1990 for teams to be used, when some of the conditions for them (notably a technical organisation of work around crews) had been in existence for many years? What does this tell us about how keen managements generally are to give workers autonomy? How far were teams 'empowered' and what were the limits to their autonomy?

4. What, if anything, would you do to tackle white-collar disaffection? How far do you believe that teamwork has 'stalled'? What might be done to reinvigorate it?

 EFERENCES

Appelbaum, E. and Batt, R. (1994) *The New American Workplace*. Ithaca, NY: ILR Press.

Appelbaum, E. and Berg, P. (1996) 'Financial market constraints and business strategy in the USA' in Michie, J. and Grieve Smith, J. (eds) *Creating Industrial Capacity*. Oxford: Oxford University Press.

Berggren, C. (1994) 'NUMMI v. Uddevalla', *Sloan Management Review*, **35**(2): 37–49.

Buchanan, D. and McCalman, J. (1989) *High Performance Work Systems: the Digital Experience*. London: Routledge.

European Foundation (1997) *Towards New Forms of Work Organisation*. Luxembourg: Office for the Official Publications of the European Communities.

Fröhlich, D. and Pekruhl, U. (1996) *Direct Participation and Organisational Change*. Luxembourg: Office for the Official Publications of the European Communities.

Geary, J. (1995) 'Work practices: the structure of work', in Edwards, P. (ed.) *Industrial Relations*. Oxford: Blackwell.

Hutchinson, S., Kinnie, N., Purcell, J., Collinson, M., Scarbrough, H. and Terry M. (1998) 'The people management implications of leaner ways of working', *Issues in People Management*, **15**.

Musgrave, P. L. (1986) 'British Alcan Lynemouth: Review of Industrial Relations'.

Osterman, P. (1994) 'How common is workplace transformation and how can we explain who adopts it?', *Industrial and Labor Relations Review*, 47(1): 173–87.

Pollert, A. (1996) '"Team work" on the assembly line', in Ackers, P., Smith, C. and Smith, P. (eds) *The New Workplace and Trade Unionism*. London: Routledge.

Storey, J. and Sisson, K. (1993) *Managing Human Resources and Industrial Relations*. Milton Keynes: Open University Press.

CHAPTER FOUR

BUILDSOC:
DOES TEAMWORKING
MEAN TEAM PAY?

KEITH SISSON

IN THIS CASE STUDY WE AIM TO:

- LOOK AT pay systems and teamworking

- REVIEW the key developments in pay systems in the UK

- EXAMINE the implications that teamworking poses for pay systems

- DISCOVER your views on the most appropriate pay system to accompany
  the introduction of teamworking in one of the UK's major building societies.

THE SIGNIFICANCE OF THE PAY SYSTEM

Pay is central to the employment relationship and the appropriateness of different pay systems is a never-ending topic of debate, reflecting changing circumstances and deeply held views. Pay has three main facets. One, most obviously, is the *level of pay*. A second is the relationship of these levels to those of other employees, which brings into play notions of *fairness* – even people who are highly paid can quickly become disgruntled if they feel that others, doing more or less the same work or performing to a similar standard, are nonetheless paid more than they are. These relationships have sometimes been referred to as 'differentials' in the case of employees in the same organisation and 'relativities' in the case of employees in different organisations. The term 'pay structure' is used to describe the complex of differentials and relativities. Typically, setting the relationship between jobs as the basis for payment has involved, on the one hand, some form of job evaluation to help to establish perceived fairness and, on the other, external comparability to help to ensure that the organisation does not fall behind the market rate. Job evaluation is a systematic (although not scientific) way of measuring a job against agreed criteria so as to ascertain its place in relation to other jobs within the organisation (Kessler, 2000).

The third facet of pay, which is our concern here, is the *pay system*. This is best understood in terms of the set of rules linking reward to effort and/or status in work. Two main types of system can be identified for the purposes of analysis, although they are very often combined in practice. Under the first, the employee is paid by time – typically for hours of attendance, but increasingly for availability – and the expectation is that a combination of moral obligation and management discipline will help to ensure that the employee contributes a fair day's work. Under 'zero hours' contracts the employer can call in the employee at short notice, as and when there is a need. Furthermore, employees can be asked to stop work (and so lose pay) in quiet periods even though they are required to stay on the premises (Arrowsmith and Sisson, 2000). Under the second, the employee is paid for performance. In this case, pay can be related in some way to relatively objective results such as physical productivity or sales or, in the case of senior managers, financial results more generally. Alternatively, it can be related to a largely subjective assessment by his or her manager of the contribution that the individual is making.

A range of performance-related pay (PRP) schemes is to be found:

- fixed incremental scales with limited flexibility, that is, there is a standard increase for the majority of staff, but the manager can increase payments for exceptionally effective staff or reduce the increase for poor performers

- performance pay linked to an incremental scale, that is, attainment of the next point on the scale is dependent on the employee reaching a satisfactory performance rating

- pay increase based on performance rating and awarded by a series of fixed percentage points, for example:

	% increase
Unsatisfactory	0
Satisfactory	2
Above average	3.5
Excellent	5

(*Source:* based on ACAS(a): 31).

Attempts to link pay to performance raise three related questions: whose performance is being assessed, how is it being measured and how is it being rewarded? (Kessler, 2000)

Historically, in the UK there was a major division between manual and non-manual employees. Many manual workers, notably in key sectors such as engineering, were paid an hourly rate to which was added some form of payment by results related to physical productivity, such as payment by results or piecework (that is, payment by item) or measured day work involving the techniques of work study to establish standard times. Most non-manual workers were paid an annual salary for a fixed working week plus an annual increment for each year of service.

A number of surveys, which are reviewed in Kessler (2000), confirm substantial growth in the use of individual PRP schemes in the UK covering non-manual employees, many of whom have traditionally been paid salaries with automatic annual increments related to length of service. Unlike some previous trends in pay systems, the public sector as well as the private sector is affected; for example, among the 500,000 non-industrial civil servants in the UK, assessed performance is now integral to salary progression for most grades. However, recent findings from the Workplace Industrial Relations Survey series, comparing the results of four surveys between 1980 and 1998 (Millward et al., 2000), suggest that in Britain there has been no clear shift towards types of payment that are based on the performance of the individual employee. Indeed, if there has been any change over the past decade it has been away from such schemes. In 1990 the survey data showed that 63% of workplaces had some form of incentive pay (either payment by results or merit pay where employees' pay depends on the subjective assessment of their work). By 1998, 58% of workplaces had incentive pay, a statistically insignificant fall. Even so, some changes in the type of incentive pay used were apparent from the findings. Payment by results was more commonly used for non-manual employees than manual employees in 1998, whereas the reverse had been true in 1990 and merit pay was less commonly used for all employees than before.

The development of performance-related pay also needs to be viewed in the context of the functions and limitations of performance appraisal (see Bach, 2000). Most commentators agree that an effective appraisal system is essential to any serious attempt to improve individual performance. There are a number of types of appraisal system:

- *rating* – a number of factors, such as quality and output of work, are rated on a numerical scale according to the level of performance, for example 'outstanding', 'exceeds requirements of the job', 'meets the requirements of the job', 'shows minor weaknesses', 'shows some significant weaknesses', 'unacceptable'

- *comparison with objectives* – the manager and the employee agree objectives at the beginning of the appraisal period and the appraisal is based on how far these objectives have been met

- *critical incidents* – the appraiser records incidents of the employee's positive and negative behaviour during the appraisal period and the record forms the basis of the appraisal report

- *narrative report* – the appraiser describes the employee's work performance in his or her own words either in the form of an open 'essay' or answers to certain questions or guidelines

- *behaviourally anchored rating scales* – the appraiser uses a 'custom-built' set of characteristics or 'anchors' derived from analysis of the particular job to rate the performance of the employee (ACAS(b): 12–18).

It is generally agreed that appraisal should serve two main purposes:

- *performance review* – to give managers and employees the opportunity to discuss how employees are progressing and to see what sorts of improvement can be made or help given to build on their strengths and enable them to perform more effectively

- *potential review* – to predict the level and type of work that employees will be capable of doing in the future and how they can best be developed for the sake of their own career and to maximise their contribution to the organisation (ACAS(b): 3).

A major problem is that these two functions of appraisal tend to become inextricably tied up with a third purpose, namely a reward review to determine the basis of individual PRP. Often this is seen by employees as the most important purpose of appraisal. Thus the appraisal system is being used both as a system to judge employee performance and as a way to identify training and development needs and so the appraiser, in effect, attempts to fulfil two potentially conflicting roles at the same time, that of *judge* on the one hand, and *helper*, counsellor, career adviser on the other. This can lead to ambivalence about, avoidance of, and resistance to the process (Beer, 1991). Arguably, an organisation which is serious about performance management will keep the reviews of performance and potential separate from any reward review. If the three processes are mixed up, there is an inevitable danger that none will be done properly. Problems are much less likely to occur where both the organisation and the individual see appraisal as a developmental process, but in most organisations this is not the case.

The development of pay systems in general very much reflects the assumptions of senior managers. One is the inherent belief – it seems to be almost an article of faith – that pay is the prime motivator in performance. The second seems to be a conviction that not only is 'managing through the payment system' the most effective means of managing human resources, but it is also sufficient for doing so. This last point is worth stressing because it has wider implications. Much is made in the human resource management literature of different types of contract and, in particular, the psychological contract between management and employee. UK management, it seems, feels much more comfortable with a form of subcontracting relationship than it does with forms of contract which carry mutual obligations. As will be clear from reading any standard textbook, however, one of the great debates surrounding pay is whether the system of rewards, in Herzberg's (1966) words, is to be seen as a 'motivator' or 'hygiene' factor. In other words, is the system of rewards to be seen primarily as a positive incentive to greater performance or, if employees feel that it is unfair, as a source of disincentive? Arguably, it is the latter consideration which should weigh most heavily with managers. In this connection it is worth quoting in full the ACAS guidelines on successful reward reviews:

- consultation takes place with managers, employees and trade unions, and agreement is reached before the scheme is introduced
- systems are relatively simple to understand, operate and monitor
- managers are properly trained and have sufficient time available to carry out the reviews
- managers, employees and their representatives are given clear information on how reward reviews will operate
- the appraisal system is kept separate from the reward review procedure
- the system is closely monitored by senior managers
- employees have an opportunity to see and to make comments on their assessment markings
- an appeals procedure is available. (ACAS(b): 30; see also ACAS(c))

THE EXPERIENCE OF PRP

Sadly, despite the outpouring of advice and consultancy available, the evidence is that in many UK organisations individual PRP schemes have led to major problems. Not only has the introduction of PRP been badly handled, the near-obsession with individual PRP means that other features essential to performance management have been ignored or not given the attention they deserve. If one sets aside for the moment the substantial body of evidence which casts doubt on the links between pay and performance, the case for individual PRP sounds very plausible. It is difficult to quarrel with the overall objective which has been described as 'to improve performance by converting the paybill from an indiscriminate machine to a more finely tuned mechanism, sensitive and responsive to a company's and employees' needs' (Brading and Wright, 1990: 1).

Equally, there appears to be nothing exceptional about the kinds of specific objectives which organisations have been looking for in choosing such schemes:

- focusing effort where the organisation wants it (specified in performance plans, objectives or targets)
- supporting a performance-oriented culture (pay for results not effort)
- emphasising individual performance or teamwork as appropriate (group-based schemes foster cooperation, personal schemes focus on individual contribution)
- strengthening the performance planning process (the setting of objectives and performance standards will carry more weight)
- rewarding the right people (high rewards to those whose performance is commensurably high)
- motivating all the people (a well-designed scheme will be motivating to all participants). (Brading and Wright, 1990: 1)

However, as Kessler's (1994, 2000) reviews of the research evidence suggest, there has been a significant gap between the rhetoric and reality in many organisations introducing individual PRP. A common feature has been a failure to think matters through in a coherent manner. Therefore, in many cases, the establishment of formal performance criteria leaves a great deal to be desired – 'objectives' and 'behaviours', which bear little relationship to work practice, are engineered purely for the purposes of having an individual PRP scheme. In the performance assessment process, which lies at the heart of individual PRP, there are complaints about subjectivity and inconsistency which, critics argue, are often compounded by a lack of attention to the training of managers in carrying out appraisal and/or the administrative procedures for monitoring. The links between performance and the level of pay are not always clear and effective – in many cases, it is argued, the amount of the incentive element is far too small to make any material difference. Few organisations, it seems, build in arrangements to measure the impact of individual PRP on productivity, or, indeed, to estimate how much such schemes cost to run.

Perhaps the most worrying aspect, however, is that individual PRP would seem to contradict or sit uneasily with a number of other policies and objectives which managers profess to be pursuing. One of these is an emphasis on teamwork. In many cases, notably where operations are interlinked, individual PRP would appear to be totally inappropriate. Focusing on individual performance goals in such situations can undermine team spirit and cooperation. At the very least, employees may focus their attention on individual targets, especially if they are artificially contrived for the benefit of the operation of the pay system, at the expense of the performance of the group or the organisation as a whole.

Why? Kessler (1994) identifies two analytical approaches to understanding managers' choices of pay systems which draw attention to the confusion of motives that appear to be present in many organisations. The first approach sees the choice of pay system as part of a relatively ordered and rational process in which managers pick the scheme which is appropriate to the organisation's needs. This approach, known as the 'contingency' approach, has a long tradition in writing about pay systems in the UK. Lupton and Gowler's *Selecting a Wage Payment System*, which was published as long ago as 1969, is a well-known example and is still probably the best guide.

The second approach sees the choice of the payment system as a far less ordered or rational management process. Rather, it is a largely political or ideological process acquiring symbolic value to support particular interests or values. In this case, the details of the scheme, together with how it is introduced and monitored, are likely to be seen as largely irrelevant by decision-makers. It is the message or messages that the introduction of the scheme sends that are important.

It is difficult to escape the conclusion that in many UK organisations individual PRP has been introduced for largely ideological reasons. The messages which senior managers wish to give are also fairly clear. First, there is to be a *change in the culture* of the organisation. It is no accident, for example, that some of the most publicised individual PRP schemes have been in the privatised public utilities (that is, electricity, gas, telecommunications and water), where senior managers were as anxious to impress the stock market analysts of their commitment to the 'commercialism' of the private sector as they were keen to motivate their employees. Second, managers are there to manage. A key implication of individual PRP is that *managers have to take responsibility* for performance management; a critical element in the process therefore is that managers have to take tough decisions about the payments to be made to individual employees. Third, and perhaps most important, there is the *focus on the individual*; the implication, at the very least, is that trade unions and collective bargaining will play a reduced role in deciding pay. Indeed, in some well-publicised cases, for example management grades in British Rail and British Telecom, the introduction of individual PRP has been directly associated with the withdrawal of collective bargaining rights over pay.

THE COMING OF TEAMWORK

At the same time as many UK organisations have been promoting individual PRP, some have also been adopting forms of teamworking. Indeed, teamworking is becoming 'an increasing part of formal organisational life' (IRS, 1995: 5). It must be emphasised that this does not just mean a sense of working together, which has always been present, but, as was discussed in the last chapter, more formal arrangements, ranging from project teams and task forces, which are essentially ad hoc, to more permanent arrangements under which work is completely reorganised, typically around a set of processes which were previously fragmented.

The reasons for introducing teamwork are many and varied, but reflect general changes in thinking about work organisation in the light of intensifying competitive pressures and increasing attention to quality and customer satisfaction. Hierarchical structures, in which the few at the top give instructions to the many below, are inefficient in separating decision-making from doing and extremely expensive in adding several tiers of managers who add little value;

delayering, in other words, has been one of the critical drivers. Specialisation, in which tasks, jobs and functions are defined as narrowly as possible, produces inflexibility rather than the flexibility which is increasingly required. Bureaucracy, with its emphasis on rules and procedures, promotes control and compliance at the expense of the commitment and cooperation essential to continuous improvement. In Peters' (1987: 302–3) uncompromising words, 'the only possible implementers' of a strategy of quality production are 'committed, flexible, multi-skilled, constantly re-trained people, joined together in self-managed teams'. The coming of teamwork inevitably raises the question of the form of the pay system. Other things being equal, it might be expected that teamwork would automatically equal team pay. Torrington and Hall (1998), for instance, note that the importance of reward and recognition for the team may go beyond issuing team T-shirts and coffee mugs. They suggest that new payment systems may be required when multiskilling is the long-term objective of teamwork. Certainly, the evidence suggests that there are organisations introducing team pay. In doing so they are typically aiming to deliver three key objectives:

- to support teamworking arrangements, encourage cooperative behaviour and underline the importance of effective teamwork

- to provide incentives and a method of rewarding improved team performance

- to relate team reward to the completion of clear, agreed targets and standards of performance.

Yet the incidence of team pay remains relatively low. Of the 408 personnel and training managers surveyed by the Industrial Society (1996), just 1 in 10 said that their organisation paid a bonus based on team performance, despite the fact that the vast majority (86%) had increased their use of teamworking over the past two years. According to the Industrial Society, the experience to date suggests that few organisations are prepared to support the development of teamworking with team-based reward, even though it predicts team

Table 4.1 Typical method of paying teams	
Method	%
Salary only	45
Salary plus payment for individual performance	23
Salary plus payment for organisation performance	21
Salary plus special one-off bonus payment	11
Salary plus payment for team performance	10
Salary plus payment for individual skill level	7
Other	4

*Based on a survey of 408 training and personnel professionals drawn from the Industrial Society's database of organisations, carried out during November 1995. Note that some companies adopt more than one of these practices.

Source: Industrial Society, 'Teambuilding' *Managing Best Practice*, No. 19 (1996).

Table 4.2 Benefits and drawbacks of team pay	
Advantages	Disadvantages
Encourages teamworking and cooperative behaviour	Effectiveness depends on the existence of well-managed and mature teams which may be hard to identify and may not be best motivated by purely financial reward
Clarifies team goals and priorities and provides for the integration of organisational and team objectives	It is not easy to get people to think in terms of how their performance impacts on other people
Reinforces organisational change in the direction of an increased emphasis on teams in flatter and process-based organisations	Identifying what individual team members contribute may be a problem, which might demotivate individual contributors
Acts as a lever for cultural change in the direction of, for example, quality and customer care	It can be difficult to develop performance measures and a method of rating team performance which are seen to be fair
Enhances flexible working within teams and encourages multiskilling	Peer pressure which compels individuals to conform to group norms could be undesirable and appear oppressive
Provides an incentive for the group collectively to improve performance and team process	

Table 4.2 continued	
Advantages	**Disadvantages**
Encourages less effective performers to improve in order to meet team standards	Pressure to conform, which is heightened by team pay, could result in the team maintaining its output at lowest common denominator levels
Serves as a means of developing self-directed teams and encourages multi-skilling	Problems of uncooperative behaviour may be shifted from individuals to the relationship between teams
	Organisational flexibility may be preju-diced – people in cohesive, high-performing and well-rewarded teams may be unwilling to move, and it could be difficult to reassign work between teams or to break up teams altogether

Source: IPD Guide on Team Reward (1996), Institute of Personnel and Development.

pay will become more common over the next two years. Table 4.1 identifies the typical method of paying teams revealed by the Society's survey.

The uncertainty of many organisations about the relative merits of team pay is reflected in Table 4.2 which reproduces the list of advantages and disadvantages of team pay as seen by the Institute of Personnel and Development (IPD). One of the key tasks of the case study will be to evaluate the arguments for and against team pay. It is perhaps sufficient to note here that a number of the disadvantages, arguably, have more to do with teamworking itself than team pay. Many organisations, it seems, remain very nervous about some of the implications of teamworking and look to the pay system as one of the instruments of controlling them.

Clearly the introduction of teamwork does raise important questions as far as the pay system is concerned. Table 4.3 therefore reproduces the IPD 'action plan' (1996) which provides a useful checklist of the issues that organisations would be well advised to consider when developing their approach.

Table 4.3	Team reward action plan
1.	Assess the need for team rewards
2.	Find out if the organisation is ready for team rewards
3.	Identify teams
4.	Set objectives
5.	Consult employees

6.	Consider options in conjunction with employees:
	    team pay; and/or
	    other forms of non-financial team reward

7.	Design the team pay scheme in conjunction with employees; considering:
	    performance measures;
	    formulae linking performance to reward;
	    the value of bonuses (bonus scales);
	    the method of distribution to team members; and
	    the rewards (if any) for individual contributions related to performance,
	    skill or competency

8.	Communicate details of the team pay scheme to employees
9.	Consider other non-financial methods of rewarding teams
10.	Conduct training in managing team rewards and team-building
11.	Monitor and evaluate the team reward system

Source: IPD Guide on Team Reward (1996), Institute of Personnel and Development.

CONCLUSION

For those involved in the design of performance management systems, there are three main points to bear in mind. First, the payment system, important though it is, is only one element in performance management. All too often, it can be argued, British management have relied exclusively on the payment system – be it payment by results in the 1950s and 60s or individual PRP in the 1980s and 90s. Second, there is no such thing as a 'perfect' system. Certainly there are general considerations to be taken into account and many of them have been considered here. But there is really no alternative to deciding what is appropriate in the particular circumstances. In the language of social sciences, there is a need to adopt a contingency approach – to adapt policies to context. The third point is no less basic than the others. As circumstances change, so do the pressures on the performance management system. A pay system or pay structure, in other words, is not for ever. Systems and structures which may seem highly appropriate in one period can be highly inappropriate in the next when products and services have changed or new operating systems and technologies have been introduced. These and other elements in the performance management system need constant review and the expectation must be that they will require substantial changes at frequent intervals.

THE CASE STUDY

BUILDSOC

Buildsoc is one of the UK's main building societies which has successfully fought a battle to retain its mutuality status instead of becoming a PLC. It was founded at the end of the last century and is the product of more than 70 mergers of local building societies. Assets in 1998 were of the order of £30bn. At the time of this study, it had around 9,000 staff in total, divided between headquarters in the north of England and nearly 500 branches spread around the country. Most of these were women employed in the range of clerical occupations discussed in more detail below. A sizeable minority, especially in the branches, were part time.

The occupational structure of Buildsoc was fairly traditional and common to much of the financial services sector. In the branches, there was an accepted distinction between the 'front' and 'back' office. In the front office, cashiers had been the main grade, whereas in recent years an increasingly important role was played by receptionists. It was in the back office, however, where there had been most change. In effect, much of the relatively routine data preparation had been transferred to headquarters which had expanded considerably to become, in effect, a large 'office factory', with jobs largely broken down on functional lines and mortgage requests going through a number of stages.

The Pay System

The pay system was also fairly traditional. Employees received an annual salary which was paid monthly. Increases took place in two ways. First, each of the grades had a number of increments. Employees progressed through the increments dependent on years of service, subject only to a bar for poor performance, until they reached the top or were promoted to the next grade. Second, and underpinning these arrangements, were annual 'negotiations' between the management and the staff association which increased the overall structure. The word 'negotiations' is in quotation marks for good reasons. The staff association, although independent and self-supporting, was by no means militant. For example, Buildsoc had never suffered any form of industrial action. Typically, the management pitched an across-the-board increase at or near the increase in the retail price index and/or the 'going rate' in the rest of the sector. 'Negotiations' would then take place with the staff association, which fractionally increased the offer or added other benefits to the package. A London allowance was paid to employees in branches in the capital and its immediate environs.

In the early 1990s, Buildsoc moved towards an individual PRP system. The initiative came mainly from the then general manager who was toying with the idea of turning Buildsoc into a PLC. He felt that individual PRP would give a strong impression of a performance culture and help to make Buildsoc look attractive to potential investors. He was supported by most of the other senior managers who, although opposed to PLC status, nonetheless felt that it would be good for both external image and internal performance. The move was initially opposed by the personnel director, who felt that individual PRP was largely a trendy gimmick which would create more problems than it was worth. He was a seasoned campaigner, however, and quickly recognised that the pressure was too great to resist and that this was a battle he was not going to win.

The Financial Sector

The context was set by the deregulation of financial services in the UK. Banks began to compete with building societies in offering mortgages and building societies responded by offering cheque accounts, leading to massive overcapacity. Simultaneously, the coming of information technology revolutionised most of the operations involved (for example allowing automated dispensing of cash), making possible substantial savings in labour costs through reductions in staffing. A sector noted for its stability was shaken from top to bottom. A key feature of the accompanying changes was a near-universal trend towards individual PRP, primarily for the ideological reasons spelt out in a previous section.

Introducing Individual PRP

In practice, the move to individual PRP involved two major changes. First, the system of automatic annual increments dependent on years of service was phased out over a two-year period. Second, there was a fundamental change in the arrangements for annual negotiations. Annual negotiations continued with the staff association over the overall increase in the wages bill, but, instead of the increase applying across the board, the precise percentage increase that each individual received was dependent on an individual appraisal in which the immediate manager made recommendations. Individuals who felt they had been unfairly treated could complain to a joint council made up of managers and staff association representatives. The appraisal system was a very simple one that involved an annual discussion between the employee and his or her immediate manager at which objectives were set based on a number of largely personal qualities such as attendance, enthusiasm, initiative and so on. On the basis of this the manager assessed the individual employee for pay purposes on a scale from A to D:.

A   outstanding
B   highly effective
C   effective
D   less than effective.

The Grading Structure

At the same time as the individual PRP system was introduced, there were revisions to the grade structure. The bulk of the non-managerial workforce was regrouped into four grades: a so-called recruitment grade; data preparation clerk; cashier/receptionist; and supervisor. In 1998, the salary structure stretched from just under £7,000 up to nearly £20,000 with a fair amount of overlap between the grades in each case.

Individual PRP in Practice

The operation of the scheme attracted considerable criticism – above all at headquarters – for many of the reasons advanced by the personnel director in the initial stages. In the early days of the scheme there were the usual complaints about the inability of individual managers to appraise properly – there had been training in appraisal but no change in the managers' own appraisal and reward system which remained geared to financial results. Many employees also complained about the artificiality of some of the objective setting, for example reports having to be written instead of being presented verbally. Some of the more active members of the staff association went further and argued that individual PRP was wrong in principle and bad for morale. Most of the operations in which employees were involved depended on close working between individuals. Trying to isolate the contribution of the individual was not only impossible but also damaging to the 'team' effort.

Added to these was the increasing inflexibility of the scheme. Originally, it was envisaged that managers would have a great deal of freedom to make recommendations. Pressure to remain within the overall paybill increase, however, soon put an end to that. Very few employees received exceptional ratings. Most found themselves located in grades B or C. Increasingly, the scheme came to be seen primarily as a way of weeding out poor performers rather than motivating the majority to improve performance. Intensifying competition in the early 1990s put additional pressure on the amount available for pay increases. Simultaneously, settlement levels generally declined with the fall in inflation, which meant that the scope for substantial individual rises became even less.

A review of the scheme two years ago led to a number of significant changes mostly at the suggestion of the personnel director, who had been preparing the ground almost from the day the scheme had gone in. The new grade of senior cashier/senior clerk was introduced to take some of the pressure off the problem of employees hitting the top of the grade. A number of the practical realities were also recognised. Precise figures were put on the amount of the awards and the staff association invited to 'negotiate' them on an annual basis.

A	outstanding	settlement + minimum of 4% with no limit
B	highly effective	settlement + between 2% and 4%
C	effective	settlement + up to 1.9%
D	less than effective	from nothing to settlement

The upshot was relative satisfaction. Senior managers felt that they had retained the principle of individual PRP and all that it entails: a clear message; managers having to manage; and the possibility of outstanding performance being rewarded. The activists in the staff association were pleased that its role had been restored somewhat. Most managers and employees felt that things had become relatively standardised in the way the new arrangements recognised performance.

The Debate over Team Pay

The decision to introduce teamwork for the majority of the headquarters staff in the 'office factory' was taken for many of the reasons discussed earlier (see also the case study of the Nationwide building society by Scott and Harrison, 1997). On the one hand there are the *pull* effects of new technology and the savings that can come from process rather than functional organisation. On the other, there is the *push* effect of wanting to promote a more demanding, performance-oriented culture. A key objective is to produce a much flatter management structure, which would allow the delayering of two tiers of managers with considerable cost savings in the medium term.

Following a successful pilot study, the idea is to devolve as much decision-making as possible to the individual teams. A programme of training and development has been decided on. Instead of being decided by a management hierarchy, it is the team which will decide who is the most appropriate person to take on tasks depending on skills and existing workloads. It is envisaged, too, that there will be closer liaison with the branches, given that the experience of other organisations has suggested that this can considerably reduce misunderstandings and therefore contribute to an overall increase in performance. The plan is that there is to be a competitive element as well. The results of each team will be published, along with figures for sickness and overtime, to allow comparative league tables to be produced.

Although there has been considerable opposition from a number of middle managers, the issue of teamwork is not in dispute. Put simply, such are the competitive pressures, that Buildsoc could not afford to miss out on the considerable cost savings achieved by other pioneering building societies. The experience of other organisations has left the senior management team convinced that this is the way forward. Indeed, there is some evidence that Buildsoc may be losing its edge in competition with these organisations.

What is controversial is the issue of the pay system. Most of the senior managers are very keen to retain the current system under the new arrangements. They argue that not only will another change be disruptive, coming so soon after the recent one, but also that it will remain important to keep the link between the manager and the employee. In this they have the advice of the old personnel director, who thinks that things are moving too quickly for the organisation to handle. Other organisations in the sector with teamwork methods, it seems, have continued with some form of individual performance arrangements.

However, the new human resource director, who has been head-hunted from the retail division of one of the major clearing banks, thinks that this is the time to move to team-based pay. Everyone knows, she argues, that the existing arrangements have become institutionalised. Appraisal arrangements have lost any purpose other than their formal role in the pay system. Her great worry is that to continue with the existing arrangements would undermine the reasons for introducing teamwork in the first place. Furthermore, the amount of money is too small to think in terms of individual and team reward.

Her own recent experience, which has involved implementing teamwork in the 'call centres' of the retail division of the bank, leads her to the view that the full benefits of teamwork are unlikely to be realised unless there is a change in focus. The fact that other organisations in the sector, including the one she worked for, have maintained their individual PRP arrangements is not a good reason for doing the same.

Instead of an appraisal-related individual performance pay element, she is in favour of a team-based 'continuous improvement bonus' dependent on a range of relatively simple, but concrete, objective measures such as:

- productivity (work items handled)
- turnaround (time to complete work taken)
- quality (complaints from 'customer' branches)
- absenteeism

together with an overall figure for team 'performance' arrived at by dividing the revenue handled by the team by the costs that the team incurred.

Conceivably, there could be some form of individual pay factor in the future but, in her view, if this was to work, it would be the team which should recommend any individual payment. In her view, appraisal should not only be divorced from payment but far greater importance should be attached to it. Indeed, she would like to see a form of 360° appraisal introduced, in which members of the team, together with the team leaders, take primary responsibility for helping to improve the performance of its individual

members. They would be unlikely to do this, however, as long as appraisal continued to be so closely related to pay.

CASE ANALYSIS – THE ISSUES

In analysing this case study you are asked to address the following questions:

1. How would you describe the management style of Buildsoc? How would you describe the role and the function of HR within Buildsoc? How have these influenced Buildsoc's decisions about an appropriate payment system?

2. Evaluate the decision to introduce individual performance-related pay at Buildsoc. What do you consider to be the advantages and the disadvantages of the revised arrangements? To what extent does team pay support Buildsoc's business strategy?

3. How do you think Buildsoc's management should go about developing and introducing any new pay system to accompany teamwork? What are the likely implications of such changes for the management of HR at Buildsoc?

4. What do you think an organisation should be looking for from a pay system?

References

Advisory, Conciliation and Arbitration Service (a) *Introduction to Payment Systems*. Advisory Booklet Number 2. London: ACAS.

Advisory, Conciliation and Arbitration Service (b) *Employee Appraisal*. Advisory Booklet Number 11. London: ACAS.

Advisory, Conciliation and Arbitration Service (c) *Appraisal Related Pay*. Advisory Booklet Number 14. London: ACAS.

Arrowsmith, J. and Sisson, K. (2000) 'Managing working time' in Bach, S. and Sisson, K. (eds) *Personnel Management: A Comprehensive Guide to Theory and Practice*, 3rd edn. Oxford: Blackwell.

Bach, S. (2000) 'From performance appraisal to performance management' in Bach, S. and Sisson, K. (eds) *Personnel Management: A Comprehensive Guide to Theory and Practice*, 3rd edn. Oxford: Blackwell.

Beer, M. (1981) 'Performance appraisal: dilemmas and possibilities', *Organizational Dynamics*, **9**(4): 24–37.

Brading, E. and Wright, V. (1990) 'Performance-related pay', *Personnel Management Factsheets*, No. 30. London: Institute of Personnel Management.

Herzberg, F. (1966) *Work and the Nature of Man*. Cleveland: World Publishing.

Industrial Society (1996) 'Teambuilding', *Managing Best Practice* No. 19. London: Industrial Society.

Institute of Personnel and Development (1996) *The IPD Guide on Team Reward*. London: IPD.

IRS *Employee Development Bulletin* (1995) 'Key issues in effective teamworking', *IRS Employment Review*, September, **69**: 5–16

IRS *Pay and Benefits Bulletin* (1996) 'Team reward: part 1', *IRS Employment Review*, March, **396**: 2–5.

IRS *Pay and Benefits Bulletin* (1996) 'Team reward: part 2', *IRS Employment Review*, May **400**: 2–8.

Kessler, I. (1994) 'Performance pay' in Sisson, K. (ed.) *Personnel Management: A Comprehensive Guide to Theory and Practice in Britain*, 2nd edn. Oxford: Blackwell.

Kessler I. (2000) 'Remuneration systems' in Bach, S. and Sisson, K. (eds) *Personnel Management: A Comprehensive Guide to Theory and Practice*, 3rd edn. Oxford: Blackwell.

Lupton, T. and Gowler, D. (1969) *Selecting a Wage Payment System*. Research Paper 111. London: Engineering Employers' Federation.

Millward, N., Bryson, A. and Forth, J. (2000) *All Change At Work: British Employment Relations 1980–1998, as Portrayed by the Workplace Industrial Relations Survey Series*. London: Routledge.

Peters, T. (1987) *Thriving on Chaos: Handbook for a Management Revolution*. London: Macmillan – now Palgrave.

Scott, W. and Harrison, H. (1997) 'Full team ahead', *People Management*, **3**(20): 48–50.

Torrington, D. and Hall, L. (1998) *Human Resource Management*. Hemel Hempstead: Prentice Hall Europe.

CHAPTER FIVE

ACCOUNTCO: SMALL

IS BEAUTIFUL?

HR PLANNING IN A SMALL FIRM

HELEN NEWELL

IN THIS CASE STUDY WE AIM TO:

- LOOK AT the difficulties surrounding the attraction and retention of staff in a small accountancy firm

- CONSIDER the extent to which small firms adopt formal human resource policies, particularly in the areas of human resource planning and recruitment and selection

- EXAMINE the model of 'best practice' in recruitment and selection and CONSIDER the extent to which this is appropriate in small firms

- EXAMINE the reasons why employees might find working in a small business environment attractive

- LOOK AT some of the specific problems facing small professional organisations as they compete with larger, well-established firms for new recruits.

HUMAN RESOURCE PLANNING

The literature on human resource planning covers an enormous range of approaches. At one end of the spectrum are sophisticated mathematical techniques to assess demand and supply and, at the other end, a more pragmatic assessment of the potential of different approaches to finding staff for an organisation facing difficulties in recruitment (Liff, 2000; Atkinson, 1989). It is, however, generally accepted that the increased uncertainty of the environment, the degree of frequency of change required as companies respond to competitive pressures, and increasingly complex organisational

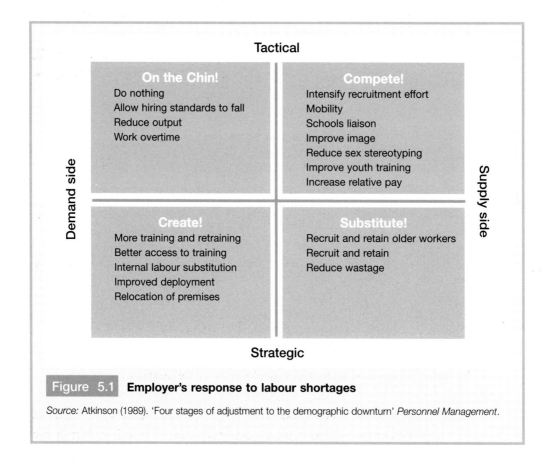

Figure 5.1 Employer's response to labour shortages

Source: Atkinson (1989). 'Four stages of adjustment to the demographic downturn' Personnel Management.

structures and labour markets make some of the more detailed quantitative techniques less appropriate, but this is not to imply that employee resourcing should be a purely reactive rather than a strategic activity. One way of thinking about whether or not responses to labour shortages are tactical or strategic is to use John Atkinson's (1989) model which shows the most likely types of response to labour shortages and the sequence in which they will generally be introduced. He suggests that there is a progression from the tactical to the more strategic and that firms will progress from doing little or nothing, through competing for available labour, to identifying substitutes and finally ending with the improved deployment and performance of the existing workforce (Figure 5.1).

APPROACHES TO HUMAN RESOURCE PLANNING

One useful model for analysing what approach an organisation has to human resource planning is that outlined by Hendry (1995). He describes four main types of employment system:

- The internal labour market (ILM)

- The external labour market (ELM)

- The occupational labour market (OLM)

- The technical/industrial labour market (TILM).

Each of these models represents a different way of balancing two strategic imperatives:

- the need to secure and gain control of necessary knowledge and skills against

- the need to manage the costs of this efficiently.

The *internal labour market* refers to the structure of jobs within an organisation where there are few points of entry, other than at the bottom, and promotion is then via a fairly well-defined career ladder. Employees tend to stay with the organisation a long time, the organisation gains loyalty of staff, turnover is kept to a minimum and recruitment costs are minimised.

Hendry argues (Figure 5.2) that a key feature of the internal labour market is the development of firm-specific skills (rather than general skills) through on-the-job training provided by more experienced workers, which

*h*as the effect of making employees more valuable to the organisation because an important part of the organisation's capital lies in their special knowledge and

The Internal Labour Market

- Refers to the structure of jobs within an organisation
- Few points of entry into the firm
- Development of firm-specific skills
- Jobs are flexible and broadly defined
- Long service is valued
- Employment security is high

The External Labour Market

- Focus is on the external labour market
- Jobs are narrow and unskilled
- Skills that are required are readily available in the labour market
- Training requirement is minimal
- Deployment is tightly controlled by the employer
- Job security is low – hire and fire

- Many features of the ILM, but outward facing
- Focus is on the external labour market
- Skills are sought after
- Jobs are controlled by occupation agreements
- Development activities are valued
- Often found in relation to professional employees or skilled craft workers

- Many of the features of the ELM, but the more extreme aspects are ameliorated by detailed agreements, often with trade unions
- Jobs are narrow and semi-skilled
- Jobs are tightly defined by employers and agreements with trade unions
- Job security is low

The Occupational Labour Market

The Technical/Industrial Labour Market

Figure 5.2 **Different employment systems (adapted from Hendry, 1995)**

expertise and this cannot be readily acquired on the open market without a further period of in-house training. (1995: 228)

In relation to small firms, research suggests that they in particular are less able to sustain internal labour markets and as a consequence they often struggle to retain key staff, and are more vulnerable to changes in the external labour market (Lane, 1994; Hendry et al., 1995).

Hendry argues that his model is particularly useful for managers in small and medium-sized organisations who are more likely to be able to describe the way in which their organisation recruits and promotes, the reasons for this and how their approach relates to the commercial and labour markets in which they operate (in other words to describe the type of employment system they have adopted) than to say that they undertake formal human resource planning.

Even so, there is little evidence to suggest that many organisations, even large ones, actually operate strategically rather than making resourcing decisions on an ad hoc basis. As Liff concludes:

*P*erhaps the most one can say with any confidence is that many UK companies continue to express a commitment to the ideas of human resource strategy and planning. How this translates into practice, however, is less clear. (2000: 98)

There are a number of reasons for this, but one of the most important is the influence of the role of the personnel or human resource function within the firm. For human resource planning to be strategic it needs to take place within an organisation where human resource issues are seen as central to business strategy, which is closely related to issues to do with the status and power of the human resource function which were discussed in Chapter 2.

*H*UMAN RESOURCE MANAGEMENT IN SMALL FIRMS

The small business sector has often been overlooked in terms of research in human resource management, despite the fact that of the 2.7 million businesses in the UK, 96% employ fewer than 20 people (Bacon et al., 1998), representing some 33% of the total private sector workforce. In countries such as Sweden, Denmark, the Netherlands and Spain, at least half the working population is employed in organisations that employ less than 200 employees. In Italy, Portugal and Greece, business is also characterised by the extremely small size of most organisations (Sparrow and Hiltrop, 1994). Even so, most textbooks on HRM contain no reference to small businesses in their index.

In so far as small businesses have formed the focus for research, two conflicting views emerge. On the one hand, researchers have presented a positive view of employment relations in small businesses, arguing that people are attracted to work there despite fewer economic rewards because of more satisfying social relations and more interesting work. 'Small is beautiful' because smaller firms offer a less formal, more personal, close working environment. At the other extreme they have been seen as nothing better than 'sweatshops' with few or non-existent personnel or human resource policies and the worst aspects of Purcell's *traditional* management style (1986) that was discussed in Chapter 2.

This contrast between 'small is beautiful' and 'sweatshop' conditions is perhaps most clearly seen if you contrast employment conditions in some of the new dot.com companies with those, for example, in small retail outlets, or 'corner shops'. In the dot.com sector employers are often highly dependent on particular employees because of their specialist skills and employers and employees often work side by side for similar wages, in a high-trust environment with limited supervision. This contrasts sharply with the employment conditions of small retail outlets where employees have few alternative opportunities for work and employers have no great need to retain particular employees (see, for example, the account of how small retail outlets have responded to increasing competition from larger retailers and the impact this has had on employment conditions in Liff and Turner, 1999).

In practice then, the context within which small businesses operate, the industrial sector, the prevailing economic environment and indeed the particular senior manager involved means that there is a greater variety in terms of the pattern of social relations in the workplace and the types of control strategy adopted than is normally suggested (Rainnie, 1989; Scott et al., 1989; Goss, 1991).

Bacon et al. (1998) comment that despite continuing scepticism about the development of HR practices in small businesses in the UK, evidence from the USA suggested that the picture might be changing.

Some support for this is provided in their own survey based on 560 small firms in Leicestershire. The authors argue that overall, while managers in small businesses had little understanding of HRM as a management theory, small business owners were familiar with many of its components and had been implementing many of the initiatives identified in larger organisations. In the majority of cases this had resulted from a change in ownership. Small businesses were more likely to reflect closely their owner and changes in control brought an important opportunity for change.

Bacon et al. go on to comment that the factors which tend to contribute to the 'sweatshop' sector:

a ppeared to include those workplaces where managers rely upon practical experience, those which are family-owned and have not grown so large that they need to recruit professional managers, and those managed by people with limited career experience outside the family firm. The small firms that had been most resistant to change in our sample were those in which a family kept firm control. (1998: 266)

From the findings of the 1998 Workplace Employee Relations Survey (WERS) (Culley et al., 1999) we can say more about the different types of small business and their characteristics in the UK. Small businesses were found largely in manufacturing, health and other business services. The majority of small businesses (60%) only had between 10 and 24 employees. A further 28% had between 25 and 49 employees and 11% between 50 and 99 employees. A little over half of the small businesses were family run, in the sense that a single individual or family had a controlling interest in the company. In most of these businesses at least one of the controlling owners was actively involved in the day-to-day management of the business on a full-time basis.

Perhaps not surprisingly, the findings from WERS show that most small businesses had no personnel or HR specialists on site (91%) and that those businesses with working owners had a less formal approach to the regulation of the employment relationship than small workplaces which were part of a larger organisation. They were less likely to have significant personnel expertise in-house, or the more sophisticated personnel systems such as performance appraisal, incentive pay systems, or family friendly working practices. Combined with this, small businesses with an owner-manager present tended to lack any kind of formal employee involvement or representative structures. As Culley et al. remark:

Owner managers generally took the view that they were there to take the decisions, and this was reflected in the way they ran their business. (1999: 273)

In relation to recruitment and selection, the WERS findings show the kind of factors that were taken into account in hiring new staff. Motivation, experience and skills were the three most important, all being mentioned by at least three-quarters of the small businesses. The findings also suggest that recruitment practices are largely informal, with more than half of small businesses with owner-managers likely to take recommendations from other employees into account when recruiting (53%), whereas small businesses without working owners were less likely to do this (37%).

One final point of interest is the extent to which small firms seek to utilise external advice to address employment-related issues. Atkinson (1994) concluded that small firms have a low level of awareness of the availability of advice and a low likelihood of utilising such sources. Fewer than one in five firms with under ten employees had used any type of agency for external support, as compared to about half of those with between 20 and 50 employees and closer to 60% of those firms with over 50 employees. Shortcomings in the ability to recruit, both in terms of overall numbers (45%) and in terms of the suitability of applicants (44%) were two of the main reasons for seeking outside help, although it was in connection with training (47%) that most small firms had approached external agencies for help and support.

On balance, therefore, the research shows that small is not necessarily beautiful. For many small firms the quality of employment conditions is not as good as large firms, they struggle to maintain an internal labour market and may struggle to retain key staff. As a result it is argued that recruitment becomes a particular problem, since they are unlikely to attract as high a calibre of employee as large firms. Furthermore recruiting just one person to a small firm is likely to have a major effect because of the small number of employees in the firm. As Atkinson and Meager argue, 'the smaller a business is, the more critical is its engagement with the external labour market likely to be, and recruitment is likely to be the most critical aspect of it' (1994: 39).

*W*HAT ARE RECRUITMENT AND SELECTION?

Broadly speaking, recruitment refers to the process of attracting a suitable number of applicants so that from them a choice can be made as to who is the 'right' person for the job. Selection refers to the process by which this choice is made, that is the way(s) in which the applicants are assessed and an appointment is made. Often, however, the term 'recruitment' is used to refer to the whole process. The relative importance of these two stages can vary depending on the context. For example, if a company is trying to recruit in an area of skill shortages, then the recruitment stage – generating enough applications – may be the main problem. Where there are plenty of applications because of an abundance of people with the right skills, or where the position advertised is particularly sought after, then the main problem may be one of selection, choosing from among a large pool of applicants.

THE IMPORTANCE OF GETTING RECRUITMENT AND SELECTION 'RIGHT'

As we saw above in relation to Hendry's (1995) four types of employment systems, in broad terms recruitment and selection can occur both internally and externally: there may be recruitment from within the organisation, for example by way of promotion or transfer (internal labour market) or externally from outside the organisation (external labour market). Organisations differ in the extent to which they adopt either of these approaches, or indeed, have a mix of the two.

Given that jobs and organisations differ in terms of what they require, some individuals will be more suited to some jobs and organisations than others. It is in this sense that we can talk about hiring the 'right' or 'wrong' people for the job. Where there is a strong internal labour market, the importance of getting recruitment and selection right is obvious, as these recruits are the people who will be offered relatively long-term job security within the organisation and as such they represent the future senior employees. But even when there is extensive use of recruitment from the external labour market the costs of getting recruitment and selection wrong can be high. At managerial level, the repercussions of the wrong decisions made by poorly selected staff may be enormous and the costs of removing unsuitable people may be particularly high. Even with less senior jobs, costs are incurred due to inadequate performance by badly selected people, having to get rid of people who turn out to be unsuitable and in the recruiting and training of replacements.

Recruitment and selection are generally seen as one process through which an organisation chooses an employee and as such often involves the production of glossy corporate materials which set out to present the organisation at its best in order to attract as many applicants as possible. However, there is a growing awareness that recruitment and selection should be a two-way process (see for example Newell and Shackleton, 2000). Individuals make judgements about organisations just as organisations are making judgements about individuals. When an individual is looking at a new job or organisation they tend to compare the information they have with their own personal expectations and ambitions before deciding whether or not to apply. If they do apply and are successful in getting the new job but in practice it was not what they were led to expect, then the new recruit may well leave their new job. This is particularly true of graduate recruits, who perhaps find it easier to find new jobs than those without such high levels of qualification. Brennan and McGeevor (1987) found that 58% of graduates had changed jobs at least once with the first three years of employment, often because of unmet job expectations. This would suggest that it is important that the recruitment and selection process involves a genuine exchange of valid and reliable information between the parties in order to establish whether or not there is a genuine fit between the two sets of expectations. The cost of failure to do this could well be that your new recruit moves on to another company and you have to begin the recruitment and selection process all over again.

THE REGULATORY ENVIRONMENT

In a number of countries recruitment and selection practices are influenced and underpinned by legislation which outlaws discrimination with regard to sex, race or age. For example, in some countries the operation of employment agencies and consultants is restricted, affecting the available choice of recruitment methods. The role of state agencies also varies, with employers in certain countries being required to notify vacancies and/or details of appointments to government labour offices. In Germany, employers have a statutory duty to inform and consult with the works council (a plant-level employee representative body) at all stages of the recruitment process and this body needs to approve guidelines. In larger German firms, the recruitment strategy adopted may well be the result of bargaining processes rather than employer decision alone. In other countries too, national or sector-level collective agreements with trade unions impose certain restrictions. The extent to which recruitment and selection is an area of employer prerogative, therefore, may depend on the extent and nature of organised labour and legal regulations. The context within which the company is operating is thus vitally important.

THE 'BEST PRACTICE' MODEL

There is no shortage of advice on how to undertake recruitment and selection. Prescriptive texts telling how it 'should' or 'must' be done are plentiful. Professional bodies issue codes of practice: for example, the UK Chartered Institute of Personnel and Development issues a code on recruitment, and the UK Equal Opportunities Commission publishes *Fair and Efficient Selection*. The best practice model presents the recruitment and selection of employees as an ordered, logical sequence of events. Figure 5.3 is based on such guidance and illustrates the different recommended stages in the best practice model. We shall look briefly at the recommended practice for each of these major stages, before examining why there is often such a large gap between *best* practice and *actual* practice in relation to recruitment and selection.

CHOICE OF SELECTION CRITERIA

Assuming that the post is to be filled (or created) rather than work being reorganised, choice of selection criteria is the first step. So

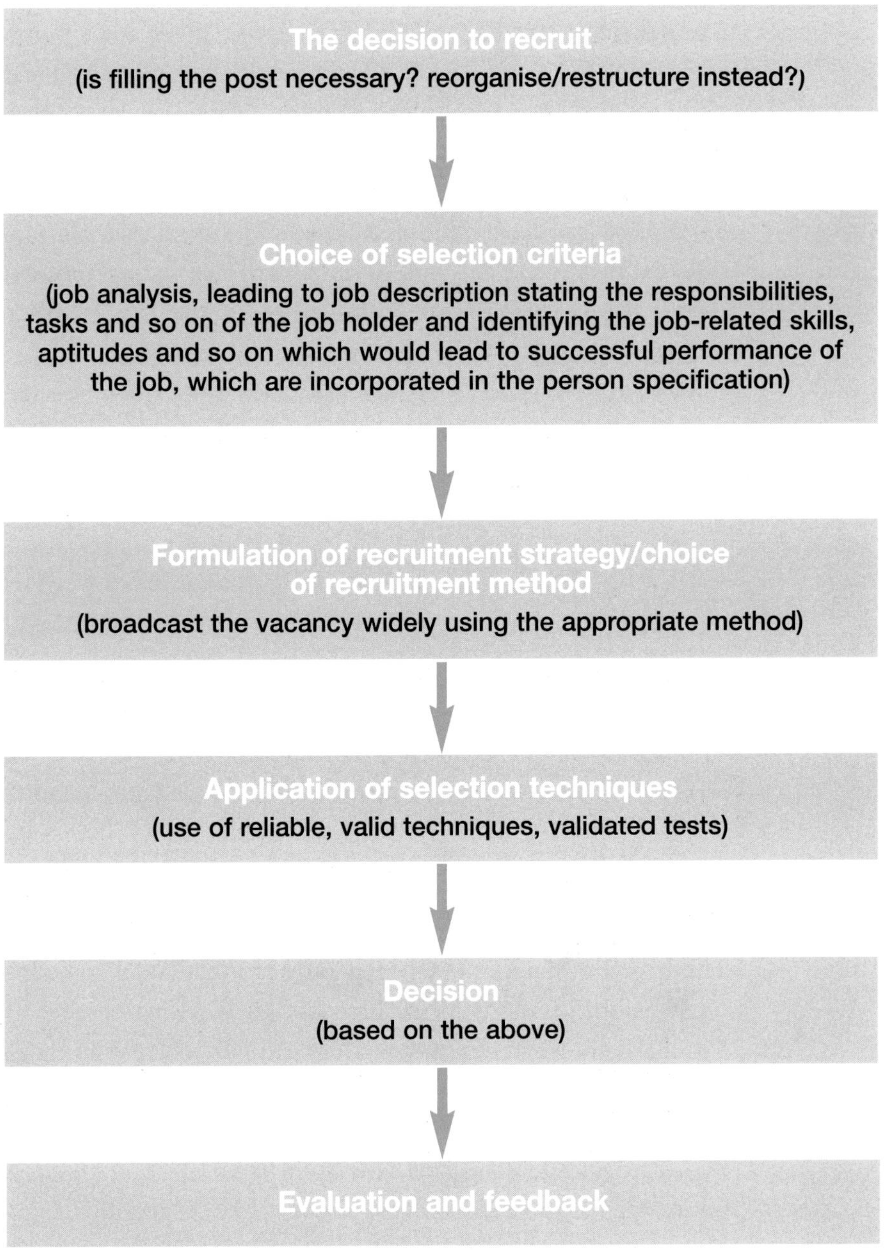

The decision to recruit

(is filling the post necessary? reorganise/restructure instead?)

Choice of selection criteria

(job analysis, leading to job description stating the responsibilities, tasks and so on of the job holder and identifying the job-related skills, aptitudes and so on which would lead to successful performance of the job, which are incorporated in the person specification)

Formulation of recruitment strategy/choice of recruitment method

(broadcast the vacancy widely using the appropriate method)

Application of selection techniques

(use of reliable, valid techniques, validated tests)

Decision

(based on the above)

Evaluation and feedback

Figure 5.3 Recommended stages in the best practice model

that the organisation knows what it is looking for, we need a job description and person specification to define the selection criteria. The starting point for this is job analysis. There are a number of techniques that can be used for undertaking job analysis, but essentially they all require the collection of systematic data about the particular job from existing incumbents and colleagues (see for example Torrington and Hall, 1998). Having analysed the job, a job description can be produced. This job description should facilitate the identification of the kind of skills, qualities and attributes which would lead to successful performance of the job as described, leading to a profile of the 'ideal person' for the job.

The best practice rules on formulating a person specification usually emphasise that the qualifications or characteristics sought should be:

- *Job related/justifiable* (for example could include 'ability to display manual dexterity' or 'stamina for working under pressure', but not 'blonde hair and blue-eyes')

- *Ability based* (for example 'keyboard speed of 40 words per minute' rather than 'good typist')

- *Measurable/observable* (avoiding vague and ambiguous terms)

- *With relative weights indicated* (some things may be more important to successful job performance than others).

This aspect of the best practice model has come under some scrutiny lately as organisations increasingly are emphasising broader organisational requirements rather than simply job-related ones. An increasing interest in personality tests, even for manual workers, may indicate that organisations are playing down the technical ability to do a particular job and emphasising instead selection criteria based on broader organisational considerations, and especially behavioural characteristics. Many organisations are looking for 'acceptability' – fitting in – rather than technical competence alone. In companies such as Nissan UK, the final selection decision rests with team leaders/supervisors. Even if this emphasis on acceptability may lead to teams composed of people of similar age, and of the same sex and race, it is seen as an important underpinning for a team-based work organisation. Allowing team leaders to select their team members fosters bonds of obligation, loyalty and mutual dependence.

Having got to this stage, a recruitment strategy can be developed: how best to attract a pool of suitable applicants in the most cost-effective way.

RECRUITMENT STRATEGY AND METHODS

There is a wide range of recruitment methods open to employers. The use of a particular method tends to vary with the level of the job being filled (managerial, white collar, manual worker) and each will have advantages and disadvantages to be considered. The best practice message is to broadcast the vacancy widely, through a variety of suitable methods, using the person specification as the basis for outlining information about the job requirements. This should lead to a pool of suitable applicants.

SELECTION

The next stage is selection, that is, assessing the applicants against the person specification. Do they have the attributes, skills, qualifications sought? Are they the 'ideal person' as described in the person specification? Again there is a wide range of selection techniques available (see Torrington and Hall, 1998). However, care must be taken to use tests that are both *reliable* and *valid:*

- Tests are said to be *reliable* if they provide consistent results over time

- *Validity* has two aspects. First, does the test actually measure what it claims to measure (*content validity*) and second, can it predict future job performance (*predictive validity*)?

Torrington and Hall (1998: 226) suggest that the choice of the most appropriate selection method will be based on the following criteria:

- Selection criteria for the post to be filled

- Acceptability and appropriateness of the methods

- Abilities of the staff involved in the selection process

- Administrative ease

- Time factors

- Accuracy

- Cost.

Employers' preferences for various types of test also appear to vary across countries. As Table 5.1 indicates, UK employers rarely make use of graphology as a selection test, whereas applicants in France are often asked to provide a handwritten letter to be subjected to handwriting analysis.

Table 5.1 Selection methods in European countries

	Sweden	France	Netherlands	Portugal	Switzerland	UK
Application form	87	95	94	83	15	97
Interview	85	92	69	97	69	71
References	54	73	47	55	96	92
Graphology	8	57	2	2	0	1
Work sample tests	72	28	53	17	14	45
Biodata	12	26	20	62	69	8
Psychometric tests	60	22	31	58	24	46
Team selection	22	10	2	18	3	13
Assessment centres	18	9	27	2	5	18

Source: Sparrow and Hiltrop (1994) *European Human Resource Management in Transition.*
Data drawn from various reports from the Price Waterhouse/Cranfield Project and ESC Lyon.

Newell and Shackleton (2000) discuss in some detail the reliability and validity of a range of different selection techniques including interviews, psychological testing and assessment centres. They conclude that very few organisations systematically assess the reliability and validity of the selection methods they use.

Interviews

Despite the fact that interviews have been found to have low predictive validity, they still remain one of the most popular methods of selection, largely because of the ease with which they can be arranged and undertaken. However, interviewers can make up their minds about candidates within the first few minutes of an interview and, instead of spending the rest of the time checking whether or not the candidate meets the requirements of the person specification, then look for evidence to confirm that first impression. Research also indicates that, in making up their minds in this short time, interviewers may be influenced by the way the candidate speaks or looks. As we noted above, considerations of a candidate's 'acceptability' may outweigh those to do with their 'suitability' for the job in terms of technical ability to perform the job. However, having more structured interviews and better interviewer training can help to minimise the subjectivity that can creep into the interview process.

Psychological Tests

Psychological tests have increased in popularity over the last decade. However, their use has not been without some controversy. For example, as Newell and Shackleton (2000) point out, in relation to cognitive testing, while it is not surprising that levels of general intelligence do play a part in predicting job performance, for most jobs the range of intelligence of those applying for the job is likely to be quite narrow. It is rare to find someone with an IQ of 90 applying for a job as a head teacher in a school, and probably as rare to find someone with an IQ of 140 applying for the job of school caretaker. Furthermore, cognitive tests can be biased against certain groups which raises substantial ethical, social and legal questions. Personality measures have been dismissed by some writers as being totally useless for selection purposes (Blinkhorn and Johnson, 1990) and, while not everyone would agree with such a sweeping statement, problems with measuring personality and the fact that job situations often present strong organisational pressures, such that differences between individuals' behaviour are minimal, mean that to date such measures have not been good predictors of future performance. A further problem relates to the wider ethical issues about using such tests. Individuals who have taken a test have a right to the results of those tests under the code of ethics of the British Psychological Society and the Chartered Institute of Personnel & Development. Yet research suggests that a significant minority of companies using such tests fail to provide the results to candidates.

Assessment Centres

Despite the growing use of assessment centres for both graduate and managerial jobs, research has shown surprisingly low validity for assessment centres, even though the validity of different components of an assessment centre are often high. This is thought to be largely due to the inability of those managers carrying out the assessment to assess accurately specific abilities required during particular exercises. In other words, candidates' ratings tend to be influenced by overall task performance on a particular exercise rather than the individual elements that go to make up the complete task (Iles, 1992).

THE APPOINTMENT DECISION

The aim of using selection techniques is to make a decision about who to appoint, or indeed not to appoint if the process has not produced someone who met the criteria.

EVALUATION AND FEEDBACK

The final stage in the flow chart was evaluation and feedback. Once the person appointed has been in post for a suitable amount of time the correctness or accuracy of the decision should be assessed (does s/he perform in the job as predicted) and any modification which may be needed to the process or methods of recruitment and selection noted.

THE REALITY OF RECRUITMENT AND SELECTION

As mentioned above, the reality of recruitment and selection is often very different from the best practice model described above. Some of the key differences are:

- The missing out of stages in the flow chart

- The use of irrelevant (that is, not job-related) criteria

- The use of informal rather than formal methods

- The use of arbitrary selection filters and non-valid tests

- The use of untrained recruiters acting on subjective judgement and personal prejudices.

Missing Steps

The stage that is most frequently omitted is the final stage in the flow chart, evaluation and feedback. This is not a well-developed process within most organisations. All too often high levels of staff turnover are either seen as normal, or taken as reflecting the characteristics of those leaving, rather than having anything to do with the recruitment and selection process. Very few companies in the UK have 'exit interviews' to find out why people are leaving. Such interviews might indicate, for example, that the job was presented inaccurately to the individual, or required skills or attributes which were not actually sought.

Another frequently missed step is that of job analysis. A number of organisations seem to jump this step and advertise the vacancy first. Research suggests that as many as 50% of UK organisations actually fail to use job analysis as a basis for recruitment and selection. This is important because where no job analysis has been undertaken the job description and person specification often become based (either explicitly or implicitly) on the person who had the job before. Thinking of jobs in terms of the people who currently occupy them can lead to the perpetuation of gendering jobs and reinforces the division between 'men's work' and 'women's work'.

In relation to small firms, there is also some evidence to suggest that rather than the recruitment process commencing with the identification of a vacancy and ending with the identification of a suitable candidate, the process actually works in reverse, so that the existence of a suitable recruit often acts as the catalyst for a vacancy to be created (Atkinson and Storey, 1994).

Irrelevant Selection Criteria

In practice, a lot of non-job related factors are included in selection criteria. Among these are age, gender, class, race, religion and marital status. Whether such criteria are stated explicitly will depend in part on the legal context. In the UK, unlike France and the USA for example, employers are not prohibited from stating age preferences and often do so. Even where some selection criteria are outlawed it does not mean that they cease to be relevant in practice. For example, in the UK selection criteria based on both sex and race are outlawed. In practice, however, research shows that discrimination on these grounds continues because such factors are often built into people's perceptions about the 'ideal candidate' for specific job vacancies. In addition, race and gender preferences can creep in at the stage where candidates are evaluated against the person specification. This happens where candidates are assessed, not as individuals against the person specification, but as members of a group thought to display certain characteristics. For example, an organisation might be looking for candidates who display 'stability and reliability', which could lead to women being rejected because of a stereotype of women as less reliable. You can no doubt think of your own stereotypes which may inform decision-making.

Informal Methods

A search for a wide pool of applicants using a variety of suitable methods does not always take place. If we look at the use of informal recruitment methods where employers use their employees to advertise the vacancy among their friends and families, there can be some definite advantages. Research (Maguire, 1986) suggests that employers can benefit from using this method because it is likely to attract applicants who will fit into the existing social organisation at the workplace, fit in with existing employees and be amenable to the nature of managerial control. Employees in turn may well then be involved in managing the new recruits, in that they take on some responsibility for the satisfactory performance of those they have recommended, using local and personal knowledge to motivate or control new recruits and supplementing managerial control with familial control. Further, the dependence of several family members on the same employer may lessen the likelihood of worker resistance. In some countries, such as Italy, it is commonly acknowledged that family, political and professional contacts and patronage are what really matters in securing certain appointments, whatever the formal position. Advantages, however, may depend on particular labour market circumstances and cannot be taken for granted. There are of course also potential disadvantages to this approach, including the problem of attracting new applicants who are the same as existing employees, rather than bringing in people with new skills and abilities. Informal methods may leave a pool of suitable recruits untapped and may also leave the firm open to accusations of indirect discrimination against disadvantaged groups.

Arbitrary Filters and Non-valid Tests

Some of the irrelevant criteria mentioned earlier, such as requiring applicants to be within a narrow age band, may be used as arbitrary screening devices, an apparently cost-effective way of reducing the size of the recruitment pool. Anecdotes suggest that other arbitrary filters are commonly used. For example, whether your application is word-processed or handwritten, or the colour of the notepaper used may determine whether or not you are in or out of the pool of applicants in some organisations. The failure of many organisations to undertake validation of their selection techniques was mentioned above.

EXPLAINING THE GAP

One possible explanation for the gap between the best practice model as outlined in many textbooks and actual organisational practice is ignorance of the best practice model, which may well be the case in small organisations which have no specialist personnel or human resource manager. However, for many organisations, small as well as large, there are other explanations for the failure to follow the various steps outlined above.

Although human resource managers often play some role in recruitment and selection procedures, the final decision often rests with the line manager. Collinson's (1987) research revealed that even in organisations with well-developed procedures based on the best practice model, at the end of the day decisions may be in the hands of line managers who choose to select according to 'personal judgement', 'experience' and 'gut feeling', which in practice can mean stereotypes and prejudice. But even where the human resource function retains a say in the selection decision, reasons of personal career interests or relative power may lead them to condone practices which are contrary to the best practice model.

In addition, some organisations may have a systematic, rational approach to recruitment and selection, but one which nevertheless differs from the standard best practice model, since there may be advantages to the organisation in not following this model, as we saw in relation to the use of informal or 'word-of-mouth' recruitment strategies. As we have emphasised elsewhere in this book, there is likely to be a problem with any model which claims universal applicability, as best practice models tend to do. The extent to which companies diverge from it may be a function of the different product markets within which they operate, as well as their differing size, organisational resources, competitive strategies and so on. Although research reveals little evidence of the adoption of the best practice model in small firms (Carroll et al., 1999), not all small firms will approach recruitment and selection in this way. While word-of-mouth recruitment methods may be common in traditional manufacturing and service sectors, there is evidence of more widespread use of formal methods in high-tech sectors even among small firms.

THE CASE STUDY

ACCOUNTCO

Accountco is a small accountancy firm based in the south of England. There are 4 partners and 25 staff, 5 of whom are employed in secretarial and support roles. The firm is over 50 years old and has a solid reputation in the local area. The firm does not have a specialist personnel department. There is a partner designated to supervise the contractors who are employed by the firm to manage pensions and payroll issues, but there is little or no coordination of activities in other areas.

Accountco is having problems both in recruiting new graduates to work for the company and in retaining its existing staff, when much better terms and conditions of employment are being offered by large London-based firms. In other words, the biggest problem for Accountco is in attracting a sufficiently large pool of applicants from which to select and the partners are now thinking carefully about what is it that will attract new recruits to apply to the firm.

Although inevitably some rules have developed over the years, there is still a remarkable absence of rigid rules and practices. Work continues to be organised largely through informal systems of consultation within which Adam Smith as founder and senior partner and his brother John play key roles. This has helped to maintain the culture of a small family firm where personalities matter more than 'plans', 'structures' or 'hierarchies'. There are no formal meetings, except a monthly partners' meeting, where they share information about what is happening in relation to any large client accounts. Otherwise communication is informal and ad hoc. While there is the opportunity to experience a wide range of activities (if not a wide range of clients) this again tends to happen on a very ad hoc basis without any formal planning or discussions. The firm has been very good in supporting trainee accountants in terms of paying exam fees, but very little study leave has been offered.

Tom Steele, one of the newest partners, is a strong supporter of the need to professionalise, to tap into the university graduate recruitment fairs and gain access to the brighter students at some of the top management schools. Tom believes that the firm should be looking to extend its client base, develop new areas of expertise and generally enhance its reputation in the marketplace. He believes that it is imperative to develop a more positive profile in the trade press – magazines such as *Accountancy Today* – without which he believes it will be impossible to attract and retain individuals of sufficient dynamism to generate the enhanced reputation he feels is necessary. Tom has also heard from some of his friends working in the United States of some of the more aggressive approaches to recruitment that are being adopted there. He is particularly attracted by the idea of recruiting on-line. As one article he has read put it:

*W*ith so many firms competing for a limited number of skilled candidates, savvy small businesses are launching what amounts to guerrilla recruiting strategy, an approach that is defining the way small businesses capture talent. Employers are realizing that they must actively market and brand their companies to attract the most highly qualified talent – quickly and cost effectively. The solution of choice? Recruiting online where smaller firms can reach and 'meet' more candidates. (Abraham and Newcorn, 2000)

However, the authors also warn that in order for this approach to be successful the firm will need to consider the following questions:

- What is your company culture?
- Who is your target audience?
- What is it that makes your company unique?

Tom is not sure whether the partners can agree on the answers to these questions. Furthermore, Tom does not know anything about the internet or how to go about recruitment and selection, let alone what a good on-line recruitment and selection process would look like. In the past he had been involved in interviews, although, looking back, more time seemed to have been spent discussing rugby and golf than accountancy skills.

Tom has done some research into the accountancy labour market and has prepared a report for the other partners which highlights the following facts. According to a survey by Robert Half International (Messmer, 2000), accountants averaged a 4.5% pay increase in 1999, the best for five years, but the market was stabilising and this figure would probably not be sustained. Forecasts showed a likely slowdown over the year to around 3.7%, but this was still well ahead of inflation.

Demand for accountants remains strongest in professional practice, with just under a third of firms looking to increase in size (31%). The weakest area of growth was in the public sector where 20% of employers would be looking to shed accountancy staff. Of the salary rises given, nearly half include some element of merit increase or performance-related pay. Profit and share option schemes occur in a minority of organisations, principally the largest companies and in the finance sector. Contributory pensions remain the most popular benefit operated by more than three-quarters of employers. Private medical cover is offered by three-quarters of all organisations, although two-thirds of those restrict the benefits to senior employees only. Company cars are continuing to decline in status, with many companies offering cash alternatives, depending on seniority. Only 12% of newly qualified accountants qualify for a car or a cash alternative. In terms of family friendly policies, a third of employers now offer paternity rights – an average of five days –

and 15% of companies offer additional leave or other benefits to support maternity rights. However, only 3% of organisations provide crèche facilities. Relocation packages are low, but study packages continue to be generous. Nearly all employers (85%) help trainee accountants to pay for professional exam fees and textbooks and also offer generous study leave. The average amount of study leave is 8 days rising to 17 days in professional practice. One important trend among the large companies has been the offer of flexible remuneration packages. Employees can select from a menu of items such as salary, holiday, time off, cash or company car or the ability to work from home. Around 10% of companies are now offering this approach. Although more than a quarter of companies (26%) have formal policies on flexible working, mainly by providing flexible hours, there is still a tendency to work for long hours, weekends and not to take full holiday entitlement. The average working week is 46 hours. Employers are still reporting difficulties in recruiting employees with relevant experience. Over the past year, problems in recruiting qualified and senior staff have taken over from those in recruiting part- and newly qualified accountants. 'Relevant experience' is top of the list in recruitment criteria, just slightly ahead of 'technical ability'. This is followed by 'communication skills', 'qualifications' and 'commercial acumen'. IT literacy is expected but not highly valued.

Tom thinks that the firm should find some help in dealing with their human resource problems, but knows that Adam Smith believes that they can deal with everything themselves. Tom has approached you to do a presentation to the partners about the benefits of professionalising their approach to human resource management in general and their recruitment and selection difficulties in particular.

CASE ANALYSIS – THE ISSUES

You are asked to address the following questions in the light of Tom Steele's concerns and the information in the background briefing:

1. What benefits are Accountco likely to see from having a more strategic approach to human resource planning? What particular problems are Accountco going to have in adopting a more strategic approach, given its size and the nature of the labour market in which it operates?

2. In terms of Hendry's model of employment systems, how would Accountco currently be described? Is this an appropriate employment system to have in the circumstances?

3. What would your advice be in terms of the actual steps that Accountco could take in trying to attract a larger pool of applicants? To what extent would this help to resolve problems with retention?

4. What sort of benchmarks would you use for assessing the 'success' or 'failure' of any new recruitment or resourcing strategy?

REFERENCES

Abraham, K. and Newcorn, C. (2000) 'Online recruiting – a powerful tool for businesses', *The National Public Accountant*, 45(6): 32–5.

Atkinson, J. (1989) 'Four stages of adjustment to the demographic downturn', *Personnel Management*, August, pp. 20–4.

Atkinson, J. (1994) 'Labour market support and guidance for small business' in Atkinson, J. and Storey, J. (eds) *Employment, The Small Firm and the Labour Market*. London: Routledge.

Atkinson, J. and Meager, N. (1994) 'Running to stand still: the small firm in the labour market' in Atkinson, J. and Storey, J. (eds) *Employment, The Small Firm and the Labour Market*. London: Routledge.

Atkinson, J. and Storey, J. (1994) 'Small firms and employment' in Atkinson, J. and Storey, J. (eds) *Employment, The Small Firm and the Labour Market*. London: Routledge.

Bacon, N., Ackers, P., Storey, J. and Coates, D. (1998) 'It's a small world: managing human resources in small businesses' in Mabey, C. , Salaman, G. and Storey, J. (eds) *Strategic Human Resource Management: A Reader*. London: Sage.

Blinkhorn, S. and Johnson, C. (1990) 'The insignificance of personality testing', *Nature*, **348**: 671–2.

Brennan, J. and McGeevor, P. (1987) *CNNA Graduates: Their Employment and Their Experience After Leaving College*. London: CNAA Development Services Publication, No. 13.

Carroll, M., Marchington, M., Earnshaw, J. and Taylor, S. (1999) 'Recruitment in small firms: processes, methods and problems', *Employee Relations*, **21**(3): 236–50.

Collinson, D. (1987) 'Who controls selection?', *Personnel Management*, May, pp. 32–5.

Cully, M., Woodland, S., O'Reilly, A. and Dix, G. (1999) *Britain at Work as Depicted by the 1998 Workplace Employer Relations Survey*. London: Routledge.

Goss, D. (1991) *Small Business and Society*. London: Routledge.

Hendry, C. (1995) *Human Resource Management: A Strategic Approach to Management*. Oxford: Butterworth Heinemann.

Hendry, C., Arthur, M.B. and Jones, A.M. (1995) *Strategy Through People – Adaptation and Learning in the Small–Medium Enterprise*. Routledge, London.

Iles, P. (1992) 'Centres of excellence? Assessment and development centres, managerial competencies and HR strategies', *British Journal of Management*, **3**(2): 79–90.

Lane, D.A. (ed.) (1994) 'People management in small and medium sized enterprises', *Issues in People Management*, Report No.8, Institute of Personnel and Development, London.

Liff, S. (2000) 'Manpower or human resource planning – what's in a name?' in Bach, S. and Sisson, K. (eds) *Personnel Management: A Comprehensive Guide To Theory and Practice*, 3rd edn. Oxford: Blackwell.

Liff, S. and Turner, S. (1999) 'Working in a corner shop: are employee relations changing in response to competitive pressures?', *Employee Relations*, **21**(4): 418–29.

Maguire, M. (1986) 'Recruitment as a means of control' in Purcell, K. (ed.) *The Changing Experience of Employment*. London: British Sociological Association.

Messmer, M. (2000) 'What does it take to attract top financial talent?', *The National Public Accountant*, **45**(9): 20–1.

Newell, S. and Shackleton, V. (2000) 'Recruitment and selection', in Bach, S. and Sisson, K. (eds) *Personnel Management: A Comprehensive Guide To Theory and Practice*, 3rd edn. Oxford: Blackwell.

Purcell, J. (1986) 'Employee relations autonomy within a corporate culture', *Personnel Management*, February.

Rainnie, A. (1989) *Industrial Relations in Small Firms: Small isn't Beautiful*. London: Routledge.

Scott, M., Roberts, I., Holroyd, G. and Sawbridge, D. (1989) 'Management and industrial relations in small firms', *Department of Employment Research Paper*, Employment Department Publication, 70.

Sparrow, P. and Hiltrop, J. (1994) *European Human Resource Management in Transition*. London: Prentice Hall.

Torrington, D. and Hall, L. (1998) *Human Resource Management*. London: Prentice Hall.

CHAPTER SIX

MULTICO: NEW TECHNOLOGY AND THE SALESFORCE

INTRODUCING TECHNICAL CHANGE IN A NON-UNION ENVIRONMENT

HELEN NEWELL AND CAROLINE LLOYD

IN THIS CASE STUDY WE AIM TO:

- LOOK AT the introduction of new technology in the salesforce of a non-unionised pharmaceutical company

- CONSIDER the reasons for introducing the new technology

- CONSIDER the extent to which employees were involved in decisions about the new technology

- CONSIDER the impact that the new technology had on the organisation and the content of the work of the sales representatives.

*I*NTRODUCING TECHNICAL CHANGE

Technical change is now a fact of organisational life for employees in most advanced industrial countries. Many technical changes take place incrementally over many years, and adaptation to change tends not to be seen or experienced as problematic by either managers or the workforce. In such cases, the management of change remains largely in the hands of line managers as part of their day-to-day operational duties. However, radical technical changes are likely to require more concentrated and significant change processes in areas such as managerial roles, organisational structure, training, skills, staffing levels and employee communications, and therefore specialist human resource involvement tends to be more prominent. Any change process will raise substantive issues (technical, financial or human resource related) which require decisions to be made and policies to be elaborated, either by conscious choice, negotiation or omission.

There are exemplar cases where human resource specialists are centrally involved in the management of organisational aspects of technical change, and there is plenty of research evidence to show that HRM considerations in technical change are being taken very seriously indeed. HRM considerations are likely to permeate technically based organisational changes if the latter are considered to be part of a general business strategy rather than an ad hoc development, and involve staff deployment issues critical to delivering the business objectives of the business strategy. This is particularly so where HR is seen to be an important part of every managers' job and not the particular remit of HR specialists, or alternatively where HR specialists have the role of 'change-makers'.

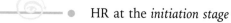

HR at the *initiation stage*

When IT investment is perceived as strategic it tends to be within a decision-making perspective that prioritises concerns of the product market over labour supply. The degree of involvement of the HR specialist will depend to a large extent on the nature and role of the HR function within any particular organisation (Storey, 1992). The 'regulator' style of the human resource specialist is seen as primarily concerned with issues at the end of the decision-making chain. Hence involvement at the initiation stage is often seen as inappropriate or unnecessary. Where IT investment is regarded as routine, HR specialists have no 'natural' involvement in what are taken-for-granted operating decisions of line management. Potentially a highly proactive, interventionist role could be envisaged for HR specialists in a 'change-maker' role, but in practice there are few examples of this.

- HR at the *implementation* stage
  Much depends on the reactions of employees. 'Regulators' may become involved in negotiations concerning technical change in an organisation where levels of union membership are high. However, many employees have welcomed rather than resisted IT, regarding its benefits as outweighing its potential costs. Because of this many trade unions have had their potential bargaining position undermined, and any negotiation over IT has been the exception rather than the rule, again excluding the 'regulator' type specialist from involvement. Where there has been informal resistance from employees over IT implementation, this has largely been interpreted as a workflow systems problem and thus the responsibility of line management rather than HR.

Where managements have sought through consultation, team-building and training to develop employee commitment and optimal utilisation of new technologies, this has often been in the context of devolved HR management. In these circumstances, HRM considerations in relation to technical change are considered to be important, although they are rarely tackled in the systematic way that the textbooks suggest.

EMPLOYEE INVOLVEMENT

The importance of human resource issues and the way in which decisions about them are made are likely to vary from organisation to organisation and from technology to technology. However, the process of implementation and the extent of employee involvement or consultation is likely to have an impact on the response of employees to the technology and the way that jobs are changed to incorporate the technology. If there is a top-down approach with a lack of employee or human resource function involvement, there may be little consideration of the way that technological change may impact on work organisation, content and levels of control. If this is the case, we might expect to find not only that the organisation faces problems in gaining workforce acceptance of these changes, but also that the change initiatives, developed without reference to the employees themselves, may not be the most appropriate ones, or may have unforeseen implications for working conditions.

Furthermore, in many organisations researchers have noted that the introduction of computer-based information systems has been accompanied by high levels of personnel surveillance directed at individual employees (Sewell and Wilkinson, 1992). The technology which assists in the day-to-day operations of work also provides the basis for collecting detailed information about the performance of the individuals who use it. In these circumstances we might expect employees to be very wary of this new technology.

For most managers the issues of communication and employee involvement are not ends in themselves. Gaining employee commitment and making the best use of the full repertoire of human resources ultimately depends on individual employees, not just managers, understanding the aims of the organisation and their place in it. Communicating with the workforce and getting a degree of employee involvement in their work that goes beyond the instrumental attitude of 'I'm only here for the money' are therefore crucial components of the management of human resources.

It is useful to distinguish between different types of involvement policies; *task-centred and power-centred methods* and *direct and indirect methods*. Task-centred methods operate at the level of the job and are primarily concerned with the structure and performance of the operational work situation. This is closely related to issues around the managerial design of jobs and production strategies. In contrast, power-centred methods are concerned with more fundamental issues of managerial authority and decision-making which determine the framework or environment within which decisions have to be made. Direct methods describe the direct involvement of individual employees whereas indirect methods make use of employee representatives, such as trade unions. Thus teamworking can be described as a task-centred/direct method of employee involvement, whereas collective bargaining would be described as a power-centred/indirect method.

Generally speaking, employee involvement schemes involve a two-way flow of ideas and responsibility. But this two-way flow is primarily designed to meet a range of employer objectives:

- to enhance productivity by increasing employee commitment

- to enhance quality by eliciting employee knowledge of production

- to head off challenges to managerial authority

- to discourage union membership

- to demonstrate a commitment to moral or democratic objectives.

Employee involvement not only reflects a variety of goals, it also finds expression in a range of different forms. For example:

- *Teamworking:* in its purest form this involves workers designing and preparing their own work schedules, and monitoring and controlling their own tasks. In this formulation employee involvement is seen as having a powerful motivational effect, both through empowerment of the individual – feelings of responsibility and task significance – and through the informal discipline and group dynamics which small teams can bring to their work.

- *Quality circles:* this technique involves workers voluntarily taking part in regular discussions on the quality of work and seeking ways to improve it. The basic idea is that 'building in' quality is better than 'inspecting' it in – the latter being wasteful of resources and ultimately ineffective.

- *Joint consultation:* in many firms, most notably ICI in the UK, joint consultation committees (JCCs) provide a useful forum for managers and employee representatives (although not necessarily trade union representatives) to discuss matters of mutual interest. In the weakest variant of this form, discussions may extend only to car parking and canteens, but in some firms the JCC may take on a powerful role which replaces or competes with collective bargaining by trade unions. In the run-up to the European market, innovative procedures for consulting employee representatives on a transnational basis were introduced by a small, but growing number of major European multinationals. Since then, the European Works Council Directive has made such arrangements compulsory for all European multinationals of 'Community scale' (those with 1,000 or more employees within the European Community) and with significant operations (more than 100 employees) in at least two member states (see Hall et al., 1992).

- *Collective bargaining with trade unions:* from the employer's point of view recognising trade unions can assist in involving employees in decision-making processes and opening channels for communication. However, many employers see the constraints of managing employee relations through trade unions as too restrictive and time consuming.

INTRODUCING TECHNICAL CHANGE IN A NON-UNION ENVIRONMENT

Many employers see the advantages of managing without trade unions in terms of the speed of change that it allows, primarily because managers are not then required to enter into time-consuming negotiations with trade union representatives (Flood and Toner, 1997). However, the research evidence suggests that this may not be the case in practice (McLoughlin, 1993). The absence of trade unions may be seen as a disadvantage rather than an advantage because of the importance of obtaining a meaningful employee voice in the process of technical change. Indeed, management may regard trade union representatives as an essential part of the communication process, especially in larger workplaces. Rather than having to establish direct systems of employee involvement, in other words a system for dealing with all employees individually, or setting up some kind of non-union representative forum, trade unions can be a channel which allows for the effective resolution of issues. Reaching agreement with trade union representatives can give decisions a legitimacy which otherwise would be lacking (Marchington and Wilkinson, 1996). Where change is imposed from above, lack of participation may lead to a lack of commitment from lower levels of managers, supervisors and employees (Storey, 1992).

While for both unionised and non-unionised workplaces the level of consultation or negotiation over technical change is low, Daniel and Millward's (1993) analysis of the Workplace Industrial Relations Survey suggests that managers in non-union establishments are less likely to consult their employees than in unionised workplaces. In addition, not only do methods of communication tend to be more informal in non-union firms, for non-manual workers in particular consultation is more likely to take place through informal channels, such as individual discussions or ad hoc meetings. Surprisingly perhaps, in light of these findings, managers in non-unionised firms claim that consultation is one of the most important employee relations issues (Millward et al., 1992).

THE IMPORTANCE OF 'MANAGEMENT STYLE' IN INTRODUCING TECHNICAL CHANGE

As was noted in Chapter 2, Purcell (1986) has developed a typology of management styles which gives us some indication about how different companies might approach the problem of involving employees in decisions of this kind. He divides non-unionised companies into two broad groups. In the first are large companies (such as IBM and Hewlett-Packard) who adopt a sophisticated HR approach, where consultation is likely to be more formalised, with extensive communication channels which allow individual employees to express their views directly to managers. In contrast, in the second group are companies with paternalistic or traditional styles of management, where there will be little concern to use mechanisms which operate as 'substitutes' for union organisation. Communication is generally one way and management may not see the value or purpose of consultative processes.

While this broad approach might give us some indication as to how employee involvement is viewed generally within the firm, McLoughlin and Clark (1994) argue that managers nevertheless have a certain amount of discretion when introducing new technology, whether there should be:

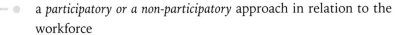

- a *participatory or a non-participatory* approach in relation to the workforce

- a *top-down* or *bottom-up* approach in relation to managers.

The top-down approach allows a high degree of senior management control over the process, while 'end users' may have little influence over the way change is introduced. Bottom-up implies delegating responsibility to line managers, thereby removing some of the direct controls of senior management. For example, the more important the technological change is perceived to be to the success of the company, the more likely managers are to adopt a top-down approach. The way in which managers implement change is likely to have implications for the outcomes of the process. For example, each managerial level may emphasise different objectives; senior managers may be more strategic, whereas middle and line managers may be more concerned with operational and control issues (Buchanan and Boddy, 1983).

LABOUR AND PRODUCT MARKET FACTORS

Of particular importance in determining the amount of discretion that managers have in the implementation of new technology are product and labour market factors. Marchington (1990) argues that where there is less competition and limited pressure from customers, employers have more room to manoeuvre. However, the strength of competition is only one important factor. The type of competition (that is, quality, price, delivery and so on) and the structure of the market (that is, large or small firms, segmented or mass markets and so on) will also help to provide the specific context for decision-making within a company. The relevant labour markets may also influence the choices made, for example a shortage of labour may encourage firms to adopt a more consultative framework in order to retain employees, while there may be less concern about any adverse effects on easily replaceable employees.

THE ROLE OF THE HUMAN RESOURCE FUNCTION IN THE INTRODUCTION OF TECHNICAL CHANGE

The results of the Workplace Employee Relations Survey indicate that generally there is a low level of involvement of human resource or personnel managers in technical change (Millward et al., 1992). Case study evidence shows that in most high-technology companies the human resource function was largely marginal or totally excluded from the change process and line managers gave little attention to human resource issues (McLoughlin and Gourlay, 1994). Legge (1993) argues that this is likely to result where the investment in information technology is regarded as routine, since human resource specialists have no 'natural' involvement in what are taken-for-granted operating decisions of line management. Where managers have sought to develop employee commitment to change initiatives, through the use of techniques such as consultation and training, this has often been in the context of devolved management. It is business managers 'eager to have a go', not human resource specialists, who experiment with non-procedural approaches to managing change.

This may suggest that bottom-up approaches are more likely to involve some form of employee involvement than those which are directed by senior management. To what extent then are line managers able and willing to take human resource issues into consideration in their day-to-day management? Asking questions about the people implications of strategic business decisions is a key element of a personnel or human resource specialist's job. If this is devolved to line managers without the necessary training and preparation, these aspects can be easily overlooked.

THE PHARMACEUTICAL INDUSTRY

The pharmaceutical industry is often highlighted as one of the few examples of British manufacturing success in high value added markets, with leading-edge technology. It is an industry where production skills per se count for little, the crucial parts of 'value added' being in drug discovery (research) and in marketing, both areas where Britain has a comparative advantage. It has a number of distinguishing characteristics, which make it very different from other manufacturing sectors and have implications for the way that products can be developed and sold. It is one of the most highly regulated industries, with profit or price controls, patent legislation and various safety standards for the research, testing, production and distribution of drugs. Governments are often the main purchaser of pharmaceutical products through state insurance schemes or public provision of health care and may also provide funding for research and development. The cost of developing one successful new drug could amount to $600m and the ability to obtain returns on the investment are highly reliant on patent protection, the acceptance of the drug by regulators, the establishment of a price and the prescribing practices of individual doctors, health authorities and governments. The high costs of research and development and global marketing ensure that the main firms in the production of new products are now large multinational companies.

The buoyant and consistent growth of the industry across the United States and Western Europe began to slow down during the

1990s. The relative stagnation of the industry was a result of a number of factors which restricted price increases, held back consumption and hindered the development of new drugs. These factors included various Western governments attempting to reduce the costs of health provision through restricting price rises and increasing the use of drugs that have no patent protection, a number of highly profitable drugs reaching the end of their patent life, and an upward growth in the cost of research and development. A major outcome has been a rapid growth in takeovers and mergers, followed by the rationalisation of production.

The global pharmaceutical industry is believed to spend around one-quarter of its revenue on sales and marketing, twice as much as it spends on research and development. Given the size of sales expenditure within the industry, it seems a likely target for improved efficiency gains. Yet sales and marketing is considered to be one of the key functions in developing the success of a company, therefore any changes in the way that it is managed may have serious consequences for the rest of the company.

THE CASE STUDY

MULTICO

Multico employs over 70,000 people worldwide producing a highly diverse range of products and having a reputation for being an innovative company. It is a relatively stable company, risk adverse with a considerable amount of centralised control. This is reflected in its human resource and industrial relations policies. It has always been non-unionised in the USA and the UK. It could be described in Purcell and Ahlstrand's terms as a 'sophisticated human relations' employer, where pay and benefits are above average, there is an emphasis on internal labour markets, flexible reward structures, employee appraisal systems and development and training plans. These conditions also apply to the salesforce, with common sets of benefits, appraisal and performance criteria and pay grades and structures set across the company.

'DrugDiv', a division of Multico, is a relatively small operation within the pharmaceutical industry. It is a 'niche player', with a particular expertise in one therapeutic area. Due to its position as the most profitable division of a very successful multinational company, it has been protected from the mergers and acquisitions taking place within the industry, although not from the pressure to maintain high levels of profitability. The main part of the DrugDiv is involved in the research, development, manufacture and sale of a range of branded products. The branded products section employs around 100 people in the UK and Ireland. Of these, about 70 are sales reps, divided among six regions, each region having its own manager.

The Sales Reps in Branded Products

The main role of the salesforce is to meet GPs, nurses, prescribers in hospitals and pharmacists in order to find out about prescribing practices and encourage the prescribing of their products, rather than their competitors. Due to UK legislation, whereby prescribers decide on the appropriate branded drugs for patients and no direct sales are permitted, no direct sales can actually be made by reps. Rather, their role entails trying to persuade drug prescribers of the benefits of their products

over those of competitors. This requires detailed knowledge of the drugs and their capabilities as well as disease processes and competitor's products. Because of this reps are relatively well educated and nearly 60% have a degree qualification. There are equal numbers of men and women and 40% have been a sales rep in the company for more than seven years. There are five rep grades, ranging from level 1 (trainee) to level 5 (around ten years as a DrugDiv rep, employed on similar terms and conditions to first line managers). All reps undertake the same basic job on their individual, geographically determined territories, but more senior reps are expected to achieve greater sales as well as having national and regional responsibilities and supporting less experienced reps. Promotion within the rep grades depends largely on sales but also on length of service. Pay is performance related, linked to a company-wide appraisal system, with a number of different performance criteria. There is no bonus system, that is, no extra pay linked to sales targets. Training provision within DrugDiv is uneven and tends to be primarily for new recruits, even though Multico's corporate policy emphasises the importance of training and development for all staff.

Introducing Technical Change

The changes consisted of two key elements: first, the provision of computers for all members of the salesforce and second, the introduction of the new database. The intention was to do away with paper-based systems to enable the use of data-driven targeting of customers, undertaken through the computer systems. Senior management within sales and marketing saw these changes as a means to catch up with the rest of the industry in performance terms and overtake them technologically through the use of electronic forms of reporting and a database for marketing operations. A new product, launched in 1995, was technologically advanced but had obtained only a 2% share of the UK market and, measured by levels of pharmaceutical sales in the UK, DrugDiv was in fortieth place. A second product in the same range was due to reach the market in 1998 and had the potential to double the size of the division in the UK and take around 10% of a sizeable market, provided they could sell it. The company believed that the new database would provide reps with the best source of knowledge about which GPs and nurses were the most appropriate targets for them to pursue. In addition, the information system would act as a surveillance mechanism; the reps had to input data about their activities each day and this could be used to help to assess their performance. The company also believed that the information provided would allow management to evaluate the link between particular selling practices and sales performance.

In December 1995 each rep was given a new laptop computer and software to enable them to communicate with each other and head office via e-mail and link them into the central computer to download information and input data into head office files. In the first instance, the data from the reps would include information such as number and type of meetings undertaken, holidays, sick days and training days. The system would feed back data to the reps on their own performance on an ongoing basis. The reps were instructed to carry their computers with them in their cars and to enter details of each call they made, including post call planning of their objectives and tactics for the next call on that target. All employees received at least three days' intensive computer training provided by the software company.

In December 1996, the use of the computers was extended by providing each rep with a database containing a target list of 160 GPs and 160 nurses for their individual territory. The database had been put together by a market research company which had asked GPs to indicate whether they had a particular interest in the relevant therapeutic area and whether there was a specialist nurse who ran a clinic at their practice in this medical area. The resulting list provided a set of target GPs and nurses which was downloaded onto each rep's computer. Performance was to be measured on the number of targets visited and the frequency of visit (three per year was considered to be optimal). Previously reps had created their own target lists, but the national manager argued that the new data-driven targeting would enable the resources of a small salesforce to be concentrated on high-potential customers.

Computerisation was delegated to a project manager with no expertise in the area, while targeting was largely under the control of the DrugDiv marketing group. Apart from arranging the provision of computer training, neither process involved the HR manager, although company policy on employee involvement emphasised communication:

*T*imely and open communication to and from employees is encouraged ... we encourage employees to ask questions, express opinions and concerns and contribute their ideas for improvement. (Multico, *UK Employee Guide*)

and DrugDiv managers responded positively to questions about employee involvement and consultation:

*W*e are very committed to employee involvement. The top line is that we are committed to the concept of stakeholders. (national manager)

*W*e wanted to involve the salesforce as much as possible and tried not to dump on them ... We try to be open and honest, we don't have [consultation] to the nth degree, but we're open and honest as to what we're trying to do. We do a pretty good job of it. (HR manager)

However, in practice, there was little concrete evidence of employee involvement for the salesforce. When questioned about this the national manager claimed that informal involvement, rather than formal processes, was 'possibly more powerful', as he received informal, ongoing feedback from all employees. This view was reinforced by the HR manager:

*D*rugdiv isn't formal, it is all about informal meetings ... We make decisions with as much consultation as possible. We discuss how much we feel is appropriate, giving the business manager as much freedom as possible. No one has the final say, everyone has a valuable input and makes the decision at the end of the day.

The results of a postal questionnaire and interviews with sales reps reflected the importance of informal systems of communication and, on the whole, communication between management and the field force was generally believed to be good:

*Y*ou are free to say anything, there are very good communications. (rep)

I think that the regional managers are eminently approachable, you can say what you feel, there's quite an open and honest framework. (rep)

However, in contrast to 'communication',

actual involvement in decision-making was felt to be poor. When asked how far they felt they could shape decisions about their work, over 20% of reps felt that their influence was quite small and a further 54% cent felt it was only moderate.

The national manager stated that a group of the salesforce had been involved in the tendering process for the new technology and that they were consulted over the use of the targeting database. However, the vast majority of the reps we spoke to had neither been involved in the decision to introduce the new information system nor in the way in which the data was to be used in practice:

There was no consultation on sales targets, it was command and control – just do it. (rep)

Targeting – no one was asked about it. Yet there are experienced reps and you are not asking them. (rep)

People with experience should be asked about what is being done and how to do it. But this only happens after the event. (senior rep)

The introduction of the new technology had clearly been discussed at some length at regional manager level, but this did not extend to include the reps. One rep explained that she had been one of three invited to a meeting to discuss possible developments in information technology, but arrived to find that the database and computer programmes had been commissioned and the performance targets had already been decided on. In effect their role was merely to provide approval for these decisions on behalf of all the reps.

The introduction of the computers and database thus occurred in the context of a lack of formal processes of consultation. Despite what was felt to be an atmosphere of open communications, the attempts at employee involvement were both partial and inadequate, in that they failed to provide a structure which would encourage reps to think about problems in a systematic way. Furthermore, the lack of involvement of any human resource specialists also restricted perspectives to narrow technical issues, as opposed to a consideration of the implications for managing employees.

The System in Action

Computerisation and targeting affected the salesforce and management in a variety of ways. The main problems experienced were software failure, increases in workload, problems with target lists, and the collection of reps' performance data.

When the computers and software were commissioned there was no one in the organisation with sufficient skills to ensure that the project worked smoothly and that problems were sorted out as they arose. The software purchased was being developed by the company specifically for the sales and marketing group and as the national manager stated, 'the supplier shafted us and we didn't get the system we wanted'. The result was that not only was the software difficult to use but that the system crashed periodically and data was lost on a regular basis. It was not until the summer of 1996, when they recruited a computer specialist as project leader and brought one of the sales reps with computing skills onto the project, that improvements began to be made. 'We now have two brilliant techies and after nine months we are getting a grip' (national manager).

Reps had hoped that the new information system would make their jobs easier, by removing unnecessary paperwork and providing more systematic means of keeping call data. Instead many of them perceived it as having led to an increase in workload, as jobs previously carried out by regional managers, particularly the collection and analysis of data, were now being delegated to reps. Similarly the use of e-mail by head office had increased the frequency and speed of demands for responses to proposals from head office.

While 45% of respondents said that it had made their job easier, 50% said that it had made the job more difficult, the main reasons being difficulty in using the computer and the amount of time involved (Table 6.1). When asked whether there had been any change in the number of hours worked, the overwhelming majority (80%) said that their hours had increased (Table 6.2) and 40%

Table 6.1 Impact of computers on rep's job

Has the introduction of computers made your job:

	No.	%
Easier/A lot easier	19	45
No difference	2	5
More difficult/A lot more difficult	21	50
Total	42	100

Table 6.2 Change in hours worked

Over the last year, has the number of hours you work changed?

	No.	%
Increased	36	80
Stayed the same	8	18
Decreased	1	2
Total	45	100

mentioned the use of computers as a cause. In the previous 12 months, nearly three-quarters of the reps also reported that stress levels in the job were either higher or a lot higher. Reps who were interviewed made the following type of comments:

*I*t's not the computers per se, although I've had difficulty getting to grips with them and I don't like doing any work on it while I'm out. If they dropped all the extra paperwork that went along with the computers it would be fine. Instead, rather than helping it is making more work, we're being expected to do lots more than we were before. Rather than the computers making it easier to do our existing job, the job has expanded with the computers. If things had been left as they were, but the computer had been introduced to help us, then it would have been fine. (senior rep)

While e-mail might have provided a possible route for consultation on marketing strategy, for example, the frequency and speed with which replies were demanded meant that responses were either superficial or never sent. In addition, some reps could not call up their target lists, other reps found that their target lists were incomplete and many reps found that the data they had input about the calls they had made had disappeared from their own territory and appeared in someone else's.

A key issue was that many reps felt that the database was at best incomplete and at worst unrepresentative of the real targets in their geographical territory. The extent to which the database could be updated to take into account deaths, retirements or relocations was extremely limited and once a target customer was listed it was virtually impossible to remove them since reps were only allowed to change 10 per cent of their target names during the year.

A number of us already had good lists, but in effect we were told they were no good and that we should ditch them. The new target lists were compiled from survey data and you know just looking down the list who are the people that have just ticked any boxes to get the free pen that went with it. You know the information's suspect, but we're not allowed to delete them from our lists. (senior rep)

The computer system linked to the database meant that the reps' performance was being assessed on the basis of calls which could not be made because the targets were no longer in the territory, were not interested in the right medical area or never saw reps. Not only did calls on 'targets' frequently disappear 'somewhere in the system', but no data on any calls made to 'non-target' customers could be stored because the system would only accept data about recognised target customers.

Responding to Problems

Despite the technical difficulties, the reps were basically very supportive of the idea of new technology. The majority welcomed the opportunity to communicate quickly and directly through e-mail. They believed that the introduction of the computers represented progress, 'the concrete face of competitive advantage', and none of the reps thought that the introduction of the new technology threatened their job security. 'You can make contact with head office and you can write your own letters, it is brilliant', 'it has made things a lot easier, you can do the admin as you go along'. However, no positive comments were made without being qualified by a negative response. At the same time, during the period of implementation, employee turnover reached over 50%. The human resources manager did not consider this a problem:

In the last 12 to 15 months we've had 50 per cent turnover, it usually runs at 12 to 15 per cent. That was because of the changes we've been making. The catalyst was 12 months ago when we gave them mobile phones and computers on the same day! It signalled that the world was changing, and some people thought 'we're not happy with this' and most people left amicably.

The reps did not share the human resources manager's view and were concerned about managers' indifference towards the departure of experienced reps and their belief that they would be able to recruit 'bright and capable' people to solve all the problems.

The reps who remained in the company responded to the problems in a number of ways. The disappearance of call data and the lack of reliability of target data led some reps to boycott the use of the computers as a waste of time, until all the teething troubles had been sorted out. At least one rep, about to take retirement, had never used his computer, continuing to send paper-based call sheets to his regional manager. Others struggled on, but ended up spending hours

trying to 'make their computers work' rather than concentrating on the job of selling. Some reps also admitted continuing to see non-target GPs and nurses, believing that it was sales which were most important and that their local knowledge was superior to the database.

Reps objected to the database information because it did not reflect their own knowledge, skills and experience. In fact, reps were primarily questioning the database information, rather than raising issues about performance surveillance. This apparent lack of concern over increased surveillance may have been due to the fact that, because of software problems, head office could not effectively measure individuals' sales performance during 1997 and there were no sales targets as such, only activity goals (number of targets visited and frequency of visits). Instead, reps were more likely to express their concerns in terms of reduced autonomy and the more directive approach that seemed to be emanating from head office.

I feel that our ability to shape decisions has been reduced. 'Head office' knows best! The rep's perspective is too limited to allow them to do their own thing, so management must retain control while trying to appear as though we have more autonomy. (senior rep)

We are told more what to do now, for example you will do x number of meetings of one type and so on. We receive messages of more autonomy and accountability but the strategy conveys the opposite. (rep)

Increased workload, greater management control over daily activities and what was considered by the reps to be inappropriate activity helped to produce high levels of staff turnover, low levels of performance and low morale among reps. These consequences were reinforced by the feeling that managers were failing to listen to reps and were not rectifying or recognising the problems that they were encountering.

The Managers' Views

Over the year, sales of the main product were only at one-quarter of the level of projections, while key performance indicators, such as numbers of calls made, had declined. By mid-year, over 75 per cent of target GPs – the main priority – had not been seen. The response of management to these problems was to see them as the result of human failures. The national manager's initial reaction was to refuse to believe that the database was either incomplete or wrong, preferring to blame the problems on a failure to input data correctly, due to a lack of computer skills or a lack of cooperation with the new system. Indeed, the longer serving employees particularly felt they were being labelled as 'Luddites', unaccepting of the new technology just because it was new technology. The problem was defined by managers not as a systems failure,

but as a human failure. It took four months for the marketing group to admit, even to the regional managers, that there were problems with the data.

*T*he targets are based on awful data. At the recent regional sales managers' meeting [held in April 1996] it was the first time someone from marketing came out and said that. (regional manager)

However, after 18 months, the national manager conceded that they had made some big mistakes; having the wrong project leader, not managing the suppliers and failing to admit to the reps that mistakes had been made. Despite this he continued to believe that there were other reasons why the computers had not been fully accepted. He claimed that people have different reactions to computers, some have a natural aversion, while others use any difficulty as an excuse for poor performance. He cited three or four reps who were keeping up well with the system, proving that problems could be overcome with the 'right' attitude. The national manager believed that they had learnt from their experiences: 'Targeting next year will change dramatically and incorporate all the learning.' They intended to purchase a new database, similar to those of their competitors, and over ten times the price of the existing one. In addition, reps would be able to change 20% of their targets and allowed more time to see non-targets.

None of this 'learning' included a commitment to involve the salesforce. The issues such as workload and increased control over daily activities were either seen as beneficial results, the consequences of which did not have to be managed, or managers were unaware that these were concerns of the workforce.

ASE ANALYSIS – THE ISSUES

In analysing the case you are asked to address the following questions:

1. What role did the human resources function have in the introduction of the new technology. What influenced the nature of this role?

2. What involvement mechanisms, if any, did the company rely on in order to obtain 'employee voice?' What influenced this approach? Is management style a good indication of how managers will behave in practice?

3. What degree of discretion did the managers have in determining the process of introduction of technical change? How important were product and labour market factors in determining the way it was handled? Evaluate the introduction of technical change in light of the organisation's business strategy.

4. Would you expect sales reps to respond to the introduction of technical change in the same way as other groups of employees? In what ways might they be similar/different?

EFERENCES

Buchanan, D. and Boddy, D. (1983) *Organisations in the Computer Age: Technological Innovation and Strategic Choice*. Aldershot: Gower.

Daniel, W.W. and Millward, N. (1993) 'Findings from the Workplace Industrial Relations Surveys' in Clark, J. (ed.) *Human Resource Management and Technical Change*. London: Sage.

Flood , P. and Toner, B. (1997) 'Large non-union companies: how do they avoid a Catch 22?', *British Journal of Industrial Relations*, **35**: 2.

Hall, M., Marginson, P. and Sisson, K. (1992) 'The European Works Council: Setting research agendas', *Warwick Paper in Industrial Relations*.

Legge, K. (1993) 'The role of the personnel specialists: centrality or marginalisation?' in Clark, J. (ed.) *Human Resource Management and Technical Change*. London: Sage.

Marchington, M. (1990) 'Analysing the links between product markets and the management of employee relations', *Journal of Management Studies,* **27**(2): 111–32.

Marchington, M. and Wilkinson, A. (1996) *Core Personnel and Development*. London: IPD.

McLoughlin, I. (1993) 'The non-union firm' in Clark, J. (ed.) *Human Resource Management and Technical Change*. London: Sage.

McLoughlin, I. and Clark, J. (1994) *Technological Change at Work*, 2nd rev. edn. Milton Keynes: Open University Press.

McLoughlin, I. and Gourlay, S. (1994) *Enterprise Without Unions*. Milton Keynes: Open University Press.

Millward, N., Stevens, M., Smart, D. and Hawes, W. (1992) *Workplace Industrial Relations in Transition*. Aldershot: Dartmouth.

Purcell, J. (1986) 'Employee relations autonomy within a corporate culture', *Personnel Management*, February, pp. 38–40.

Sewell, G. and Wilkinson, B. (1992) 'Empowerment or emasculation? Shopfloor surveillance in a total quality organization' in Blyton, P. and Turnbull, P. (eds) *Reassessing Human Resource Management*. London: Sage.

Storey, J. (1992) *Developments in the Management of Human Resources*. Oxford: Blackwell.

LONDON BOROUGH:
A PARTNERSHIP
AGREEMENT?

KEITH SISSON

IN THIS CASE STUDY WE AIM TO:

- LOOK AT the advantages and disadvantages of introducing a partnership agreement in local government organisation in the UK

- REVIEW the reasons why the issue of partnership has come to prominence

- DESCRIBE the main features of partnership agreements and DISCUSS the implications they have posed

- DISCOVER your views on how the management of a local authority should respond to a proposal from a new union official to implement such an agreement.

*P*ARTNERSHIP IN THEORY AND PRACTICE

There is no clear definition of partnership (Tailby and Winchester, 2000). Indeed, one of the major weaknesses of the concept is that it can mean very different things. Especially controversial is whether partnership is essentially about the relationship between the organisation and the individual or the organisation and the trade union. Some organisations in the UK claiming to be partnership companies, such as Motorola and Unipart, do not recognise trade unions for the purpose of collective bargaining. Significantly, too, a recent report from the UK's Department of Trade and Industry/Department for Education and Employment (1997), reckoned to be highly regarded by ministers and those close to the prime minister, extols the virtues of *partnerships with people* but makes no mention of trade unions, albeit these employees are expected to be mostly working 'collectively' in teams.

That said, partnership agreements, along with the wider notion of social partnership, imply a trade union presence. Certainly the term 'social partners' has come to be understood in most European Union member countries as embracing the representative organisations of both employers and employees, that is, trade unions. Two fundamental issues are involved. The first is the role of trade unions. Historically, trade unions have tended to be seen, and to have seen themselves, as the *permanent opposition*, challenging management's authority, as well as seeking to improve the position of their members by establishing a floor of both procedural and substantive rights. Under the pressure of intensifying international competition and declining membership in many countries, however, there have been moves to redefine relations with management and develop what have been called *productivity coalitions*, designed to promote organisational performance and hence the future employment of their members.

The second is the approach to the management of the employment relationship. In Chapter 6, the Multico case, we considered the difference between direct and indirect forms of employee involve-ment. This distinction is also relevant to the debate on partnership. A company's approach to the management of the employment rela-tionship, as we saw in Chapter 2, can take one of four basic forms. Where a company chooses to avoid indirect representation, this may take two different forms, with either an emphasis on direct controls typical of Purcell's (1986) *traditional style* or an emphasis on direct participation and self-discipline typical of Purcell's *sophisticated human relations* style. Alternatively, managements may accept, or be required to accept, the logic of some form of employee representa-tion through trade unions, in which case the relationship may be essentially conflictual, as is typical of Purcell's *constitutional* style, or it may involve 'the extension of status' and be more cooperative, as in the case of partnership agreements, which reflect Purcell's *consul-tative* style.

Marchington and Wilkinson point out that there are a number of reasons why employers should choose to work with, rather than against, unions in the workplace:

*F*irstly, management may regard trade union representatives as an essential part of the communication process in larger workplaces. Rather than being forced to establish a system for dealing with all employees, or setting up a non-union representative forum, trade unions are seen as a channel which allows for the effective resolution of issues concerned with pay bargaining or grievance handling. It is also the case that reaching agreement with union representatives, in contrast to imposing decisions, can provide decisions with a legitimacy which otherwise would be lacking. It can also lead to better decision making as well. (1996: 237)

A survey carried out by IRS (1995) asked company representa-tives to outline the advantages and disadvantages of working with trade unions. The benefits suggested included:

- The stable structure such a relationship gives to the manage-ment of employees

- Its role in the mechanism of upward communication from staff

- Its cost-effectiveness as a communication tool when compared to individualised approaches.

The main drawbacks related to the perception that unions tend to resist change and therefore it takes a long time to get things done. The result was perceived to be a reduction in the ability of managers to respond quickly and flexibly to market pressures and opportunities. As we discussed in Chapter 6, although this is a common view among managers (Flood and Toner, 1997), the research evidence suggests that this may not be the case in practice (McLoughlin, 1993).

As Torrington and Hall argue, from a strictly managerial point of view, the interest in working with trade unions

*r*evolves around the extent to which it will deliver collective consent to a general framework of rules and guidelines within which management and employees operate. (1998: 510)

THE EUROPEAN DIMENSION: TOWARDS A 'NEW' SOCIAL MODEL?

It will be helpful to begin by putting the issues into the wider European context. The characteristics of the traditional European social model or models are best described in comparison with those of the US model as this is reflected in the policy debate. Briefly, both the European and US models are seen as having strengths and weaknesses (Table 7.1). The key features of the European model are an emphasis on employee rights introduced by collective bargaining and/or legal regulation, leading to security of employment and relatively high levels of pay and conditions generally. There is a downside, however, which manifests itself in inflexibility, a lack of competitiveness (leading, for example, to overseas investment by European-owned companies themselves) and high levels of unemployment.

In most respects, the US model is deemed to be the exact opposite. Management is supposedly much freer of the restrictions of

Table 7.1 Models of HRM/IR: the current stereotypes

	Key features	Outcomes
The European model	Strong trade unions Collective bargaining Legal regulation (*employee rights*)	Security Relatively high pay Inflexibility Lack of competitiveness Unemployment
The US model	Weak trade unions Little collective bargaining Management regulation (*management prerogative*)	Insecurity Relatively low pay Flexibility Competitiveness Employment

collective bargaining and legal regulation, leading to greater flexibility, improved competitiveness and a much lower rate of unemployment than in Europe. The trade-off is considerable insecurity, lower levels of pay and poorer working conditions for many employees.

These models, it must be emphasised, are stereotypes. Patently, there is not one single US model, any more than there is one European model. They are no more than expressions of a particular moment in time. Go back into the 1980s and there would have been a very different judgement; it would have been very difficult to find any one preferring the US to the German model, for example. However, the point is that this is how things have come to be characterised at the present moment.

The 'new' or emerging European social model is summarised in

Table 7.2 The 'new' European social model

Main ingredients	Outcomes
Flexibility	Quality people
Security	Quality goods and services
Education and training	Competitiveness
Direct participation ('empowerment')	'Good' jobs
Indirect participation ('partnership')	

Table 7.2. In short, it tries to get the best of both worlds. It seeks to combine flexibility with security of employment, education and training, and direct participation ('empowerment') of individual employees with the indirect participation ('partnership') of employee representatives. The outcomes are the virtuous and reinforcing circle of quality people, quality goods and services, competitiveness and 'good' jobs.

It will be helpful to expand the key points and consider them in more detail (for further details, see Sisson, 1997). The starting point is a particular view of Europe's main source of competitive advantage in the rapidly changing and increasingly competitive global marketplace. Costs, of course, are important but developed economies, it is argued, cannot hope to compete on the basis of cheapness with competitors in Eastern Europe and the Far East, let alone the Third World. This would mean lowering wages and living standards to unacceptable levels and would be unlikely to be successful. Instead, the emphasis needs to be on quality products and services. Not only will these satisfy the growing demand for more specialised niche goods, but, more fundamentally, they make it possible to build on employees' long-standing demands for more challenging and rewarding jobs and 'exploit' their higher education and skills. So-called 'high performance' work systems not only appear to offer the prospect of ever-increasing levels of productivity, but also enable management to exploit other sources of competitive advantage such as quality and customisation. It is Europe's people, in other words, who are the key to success.

A second respect in which the thinking differs from received wisdom involves the type of flexibility being sought. Most recent attention has been on external flexibility, that is, the ability of the organisation to vary its commitments through reductions in the number of employees or changes in their status (for example from permanent to temporary) or through subcontracting. The real advances, it is argued, are much more likely to come from internal flexibility leading to improved organisational capacity. In the words of the European Commission's Green Paper *Partnership for a New Organisation of Work* published in April 1997:

*I*t is about the scope for improving employment and competitiveness through a better organisation of work at the workplace, based on high skill, high trust and high quality. It is about the will and ability of management and workers to take initiatives, to improve the quality of goods and services, to make innovations and to develop the production process and consumer relations. (p. 1)

The insecurity that much of the delayering and downsizing of recent years has produced, it can be argued, is proving to be counter-productive. For a more detailed discussion about the likely impacts of job insecurity you should read the background briefing for Chapter 9. In summary, job insecurity can lead to employees being less willing to accept change, more resentful of imposed change and more secretive and competitive (Greenhalgh and Sutton, 1991) as well as leading to depression, poorer work performance, absenteeism, alcoholism and drug abuse as well as reduced motivation (Daniels, 1993). There is little or none of the trust that managers are encouraged to seek as the basis for a new 'psychological contract.'

The third, and in many ways the most important, respect in which the new thinking differs involves the way change is to be brought about. Much of the organisational behaviour literature puts the onus exclusively on management. The new thinking emphasises the role of partnership above all at workplace level. It is not just a question of the individual employee needing representation to help to balance inequality of power with the employer. The views of employees, most commentators agree, are vital to the success of changes in work organisation. In the absence of a representative voice, there is a danger that these views are either not expressed, for fear of antagonising managers, or are simply ignored. Trust is also essential: trust depends on the legitimacy of decisions, and joint regulation is one of the most tangible ways of expressing such legitimacy. Also important is the view that the speed of change is nowhere near fast enough. In effect, advocates of the new thinking argue that a coalition for change is required which involves all the major stakeholders and not just management.

This type of thinking is not exclusive to Europe, indeed much of it was stimulated by the early work of Kochan and his colleagues in the USA (Kochan et al., 1986). It is in Europe, however, where it has taken strongest root and begun to influence key policy-makers both at national and EU level. It is implicit in many recent developments such as those under the agreement on social policy. However, perhaps its most clear-cut expression is found in the European Commission's Green Paper *Partnership for a New Organisation Of Work* (1997). Significantly, too, advocates of the model can point to a growing number of high-profile examples in other countries as well as the UK – Bayer, BMW, Mercedes-Benz and Volkswagen in Germany and Fiat and Zanussi in Italy – to emphasise its practical application.

PRESSURES FOR PARTNERSHIP IN THE UK

Although the terms 'social partners' and 'social partnership' were not widely used in the UK in the 1980s and early 1990s, partnership is not a new concept for the UK. For example, the Involvement and Participation Association, which brings together management and trade union representatives, was formed as long ago as 1896 with a mandate to promote the cause. There are also a number of long-standing examples. The John Lewis Partnership (the major multiple retailer), as its name implies, has been a long-time exponent: individual employees are regarded as partners and receive a substantial share of the company's profits. Another example is the chemical company ICI. In this case partnership took the form of a highly extensive joint consultation system, which dates back to the formation of the company in 1926, and its early recognition of trade unions; a structure of divisional and enterprise committees was set up to receive and discuss information even relating to present and future investment.

At the risk of oversimplification, however, it was the trade unions and their supporters who initiated the discussion about partnership. Two sets of issues emerged in the late 1980s. One, which grew out of the debates over the 'new realism' in the mid-1980s, involved the attempt to set a 'new agenda' for unions (Edmonds and

Tuffin, 1990). This drew attention to the challenges facing British industry and the need for trade unions to respond to them in positive ways:

The response that we envisage involves British trades unions developing a joint approach with the employers to create the conditions for economic success and social cohesion in the 1990s ... It would mean talking to employers about how to improve quality performance, cost and price competitiveness and a fairer society.

The agenda would include issues such as training ... It would cover questions such as industrial investment, R&D expenditure and new product development, and how to encourage them and promote cooperation in making them work. It would embrace subjects like the restructuring of work for maximum mutual flexibility, equal opportunities for women, racial discrimination in the labour market, and health and safety in the wider work environment. (Edmonds and Tuffin, 1990: 3)

The second issue involved institutions and the suggestion that trade unions should think seriously about supporting the introduction of some form of works council. Here two considerations have been important. One is a growing conviction that it is no longer possible to justify a system where working people have no legal right to consultation and negotiation. In the words of the British Labour Party's employment spokesperson in the House of Lords:

It can surely be argued that what Britain needs now is to involve as many workers as possible in some form of effective participation, so that what is provided is available to relatively small groups in shops, offices, restaurants and other areas where total employment opportunities are growing fast. For the most part these are places where the majority of workers are totally excluded from the decision making process and at the moment there is no collective bargaining. (McCarthy, 1988: 12–13)

The second is a growing recognition that a new institution would be needed if there was to be a joint discussion of the kinds of issue set out in the new agenda. New forums for information, consultation and participation would need to be established.

There was a positive response to some aspects of these ideas among the managers associated with the Involvement and Participation Association. An approach which stresses both 'individualism' and 'collectivism', far from being contradictory, makes perfect sense, some argued; one is as essential as the other in winning 'hearts and minds'. If there is a problem, according to this view, it might be said to be the need to shift the nature of the relationship with trade unions from the antagonism of the past to one of 'partnership' in the future.

The outcome was the preparation of a joint statement of intent, *Towards Industrial Partnership* (IPA, 1992), which was signed by a number of leading management and trade union representatives. The statement of intent starts by recognising the weakness of an industrial relations system based on conflict resolution and pointing out that management and unions have many common goals. The proposal is in three parts:

- *Part 1:* suggests that the parties need to begin by agreeing certain joint aims: a joint commitment to the success of the enterprise; a recognition that there must be a joint effort to build trust; and a joint declaration recognising the legitimacy of the role of each party.

- *Part 2:* spells out the areas in which management and trade unions need to rethink their approach. Management is asked to do far more to ensure employment security, to share the results of success with all who contribute to it, and to recognise the employee's right to be informed, consulted and represented in matters of concern to them. Trade unions, in turn, are asked to promote job flexibility (that is, give up what some managers refer to as 'job control'), to recognise that union and non-union members have a right to representation (that is, give up the long-standing commitment to single channel representation), and to accept management attempts to involve individual employees.

- *Part 3:* sums up the benefits of the new approach and stresses
  that it would enable discussion on a range of subjects which
  have not featured prominently in collective bargaining in the
  UK in the past (quality through improvement, training, education, investment, communication, equal opportunity, corporate
  values, company success, environment, and health and safety).

The proposal specifically avoided attempting to prescribe any particular model for representation, nonetheless, it did suggest two possibilities. One was to *broaden the existing collective bargaining framework*
to include subjects of wider policy. The other, which is the more
radical approach in the UK, was to *introduce 'new' institutions*, works
councils, where a wide agenda of issues could be discussed between
managers and employee representatives. In the latter case the
understanding was more or less explicit that a universal right to
representation would apply, that is, there was to be a trade-off
between trade union acceptance of employee-based consultative
machinery in return for management's willingness to discuss a
wider range of issues with trade unions.

Political developments were also important. Although the
notion of social partnership, in the sense of national-level relations,
had long been a feature of a number of EU member countries, the
completion of the single European market pushed the issue of the
social dimension to the fore. One consideration was trade union
demands for greater information and consultation in multinational
companies leading to the European Works Council Directive of
1994. Another was the desire of the European Commission to
promote social dialogue as way of developing social policy and
dealing with the restructuring that the single European market was
expected to bring about. Conveniently, too, the support for dialogue
and agreement fitted well with the principle of subsidiarity. As the
1990s progressed there were also concerns about the need to
modernise work organisation as means to competitive success. This
thinking was crystallised in the European Commission's 1997 Green
Paper *Partnership for a New Organisation of Work* referred to earlier.

The key development in the UK was the election of a Labour government in 1997. The full implications of its policies for industrial relations remain ambiguous, nonetheless there was a different climate. Ministers continually used the rhetoric of partnership in their speeches and deliberations. Critically, too, they adopted a very different stance to Europe from the previous British government, signing up to the social dimension of the Maastricht Treaty in 1997.

A CLOSER LOOK AT A PARTNERSHIP AGREEMENT

Partnership agreements differ considerably in their details, which is hardly surprising given that companies as diverse as Blue Circle (IRS, 1997), Legal and General (IRS, 1998), Rover (IRS, 1992) and Tesco (Allen, 1998) have been involved. Welsh Water is given as an example in this summary partly because of the way in which it has developed and partly because it is the agreement with which the UNISON official involved in the case study was directly involved.

Welsh Water was privatised in 1989. Like other water companies, and local authorities, it had for many years been the subject of detailed central agreements covering the different groups of employees: 'manual', 'non-manual' and 'craft'. It embarked on a partnership following the break-up of these agreements. There have, in effect, been three agreements which give some idea of the development and timescale that can be involved.

Partnership 1 – 1990

This introduced the following key features:

- replacement of the traditional annual pay negotiations by an agreed objective formula (embracing the November Retail Price Index percentage; links with the local labour market undertaken by an independent organisation; and a profit-related component)

- new structures involving a single table representative council (all union representatives agree to be present at the same meeting) supported by joint 'issue' groups

- new working time arrangements involving greater flexibility, a form of annual hours arrangement and a reduction in the working week for manual and craft employees (see Arrowsmith and Sisson, 2000, for further discussion of these types of arrangement)

- the harmonisation of the working conditions, policies and procedures of all employees (manual, non-manual and craft)

- the introduction of monthly pay through credit transfer for all employees

- a commitment to introduce a new pay structure

- a range of measures to improve productivity through greater flexibility

- a 'no compulsory redundancy' policy.

In the words of the manager and trade union official mostly responsible:

*I*n many ways, this agreement was a breakthrough. It moved the company – and more importantly the trade unions – away from the traditional adversarial stances embodied in the annual pay negotiation. The introduction of a 'no compulsory redundancy' policy also started to build the trust necessary for the organisation to introduce many of the changes required to face the new challenges of privatisation. For manual and craft employees, hitherto the 'second-class citizens' of the industry, this was a recognition that they were equally important to the success of the organisation as other staff. A further key aspect of the agreement was the method of 'internally marketing' its contents. It was agreed that this should be a joint responsibility of management and the trade unions through joint presentations. (Thomas and Wallis, 1998: 163)

Partnership 2 – 1993

This introduced the following key features:

- introduction of a jointly prepared unified pay structure for all employees

- performance appraisal and new understandings on performance management

- provisions for handling reductions in the workforce including the opportunity for employees to leave at mutually acceptable dates, and recognition of the need to consult and involve employees on how jobs would be managed in the future

- further refinements to the pay formula

- a renewal of the employment security provisions.

Partnership 3 – 1995

A distinguishing feature of this phase was its preparation. To ensure that future developments matched needs, senior personnel managers and full-time officers carried out a series of 'road shows', meeting small groups of employees covering over 75% of the work-force. The agenda embraced a review of developments, the concerns of employees and the identification of issues. The continued uncertainty about the nature of partnership resulted in a restatement of the basic principles:

What you give – sharing responsibility for continued improvements in performance. Welsh Water can be assured that everyone shares the responsibility in meeting our business objectives and improving the highest levels of customer service. What you get – the benefits of Partnership are that our people have continuing employment and pay security with good conditions of employment.

(Unpublished company statement)

The employment security provisions were put on an ongoing basis to help to alleviate fears about their regular review. The position of temporary staff was also addressed through a new review procedure.

Benefits and Implications

Benefits cited by management include the establishment of a 24-hour call centre to suit customer needs; improved quality; significant reductions in costs; customers standards as measured by the director general to be 'good' to 'very good'; acceptance of continuous change; and a willingness of employees to work with contractors, agency and temporary staff, which had been the source of major problems in the 1980s.

For employees the benefits have included greater employment and pay security; harmonisation of conditions and greater equality; training and development opportunities and greater control of their immediate working lives. Thomas and Wallis (1998: 166–9), who helped to draw up the agreements, also give a frank appraisal of the implications of having partnership arrangements for both management and trade unions.

For *management* they suggest that the implications are as follows:

- a willingness to commit the act of faith that the benefits would outweigh the costs

- a need for a change in style for individual managers – from being directors to being facilitators

- a need for greater openness

- a need for a change in approach to the trade unions – problem-solving

- employment security has removed the elimination of poor performers through the redundancy route, leading to extra strain on the performance management system

- greater activity has led to expectations of greater reward.

For *trade unions* they suggest that the implications are as follows:

- the nature of the partnership restricts the number of opportunities for trade union officers to demonstrate publicly their value to their members

- opposition for opposition's sake had to go, to be replaced by a recognition that the long-term interests of the members were best served by helping the organisation to be more successful

- acceptance of the need for joint communication

- trade union officials and senior representatives had to let go of some of their power

- full-time officials in particular faced charges that they were in 'management's pocket'.

EVALUATION

There has as yet been no systematic evaluation of the impact of agreements such as that introduced by Welsh Water. Certainly many of the participants are enthusiastic. There is also wider evidence to suggest that partnership 'works'. In the UK the IPA (1998) commissioned a survey of its members which established positive links between the principles of partnership, the practice of partnership and organisational performance. Even more widespread support comes from the report of the important ten-country study of the role of direct participation in organisational change, sponsored by the European Foundation for the Improvement in Living and Working Conditions (1997). Not only did the effects of direct participation increase with the degree of employee representative involvement in its introduction, the more extensively employee representatives were involved, the more 'successful' direct participation was deemed to be in the view of managers.

Nonetheless, doubts have been expressed on both operational and ideological grounds. On operational grounds, there are worries about the time and effort involved as compared with the likelihood of benefits. The sheer scale of the changes required is another consideration, those required in terms of the role and style of managers being especially fundamental. The feasibility of trying to build long-term relationships in the midst of so much uncertainty is yet another consideration. Worries have also been expressed about the quality of the representatives.

On ideological grounds, there remains a strong resistance to collectivism in general and trade unions in particular on the part of many managers in the UK. Unions are promoting partnership, some cynics would say, because of their weakness and managers should not be doing anything that stops unions from withering on the vine. The important link, others would argue, is between the organisation and the individual employee, and involving a trade union is tantamount to bringing a third party into what is a close family relationship. Yet another group, although they may not admit it, find the whole business of consultation, be it with individuals or their representatives, extremely uncomfortable, believing that seeking the views of employees undermines their managerial authority.

For trade unions, involvement in the kinds of coalition for change being envisaged poses both opportunities and threats. Trade unions are having to face up to the implications of the different trajectories of work organisation regardless of any strategic position they adopt. More positively, it can be argued, there is much to be gained from trade unions (at national and workplace level) presenting themselves as the champions of the 'quality' forms of work organisation and the training and development opportunities that go with them. Not only would it enable them to give substance to what, at the moment, tend to be rather vague notions of 'partnership', but the benefits, both in terms of public esteem and, more importantly, membership, could be considerable.

Yet there are many within trade unions who see partnership agreements as a major threat. In particular, they are worried that they will compromise the traditional role of unions which is to defend their members' interest. Employee representatives will become part of management. One trade union official involved in the negotiations at Welsh Water expressed the basic dilemma:

*P*artnership does mean a different sometimes a more challenging role for the trade unions. It is easy to confront, to say NO. It is far more difficult to create a new role working with employees and the company to develop a better future not only for ourselves but more importantly for our customers. (Involvement and Participation Association, 1997: 16)

More fundamentally, flexible working requires trade unions to move from the general to the particular. The worry is that, as well as undermining the role of trade unions in establishing minimum standards, it will make it more difficult to manage the tensions between members of different organisations and interest groups, for example skilled and unskilled, full-time and part-time, with significant implications for the ability to maintain collective strength.

For the moment, partnership agreements remain very much a minority movement with their wider adoption seeming to depend on the political context. There is as yet no indication that the current Labour government, for all its commitment to partnership, will actually legislate for the universal right to employee voice. Management and unions will be left to make their own decisions.

Things could change, however. The partnership model is one which fits in well with the thinking of the European Commission and there is the prospect of negotiations under the Maastricht social policy process which may eventually lead to a measure providing for information and consultation arrangements at national level for enterprises with as few as 20 employees. A range of collective employee voice mechanisms is being introduced in the UK to deal with what the European Court of Justice has termed the representation 'gap'. One way in which a representation gap occurs is where, for example, a piece of legislation (such as that relating to collective redundancies and transfer of undertakings or health and safety and working time) provides for consultation with employees only if a union is recognised. Another area concerns European works councils. Under the Maastricht Treaty, multinational companies with more than 1,000 employees in the EU and with at least 150

employees in two member countries must now introduce procedures for consultation with employees on a transnational basis.

UK management is also on trial. The relative lack of competitiveness, and the contributory role of a lack of attention to training
and development, is something that the current Labour government
is becoming increasingly concerned about. The government could
well lose patience with British management and bring forward legislation to encourage partnership.

THE CASE STUDY

LONDON BOROUGH

London Borough is a
large, so-called 'unitary'
local authority providing
a full range of services for its
population on the outskirts of the
capital city. Altogether, it employs
around 15,000 people spread across a range
of manual, craft and clerical-administrative
occupations, together with teachers and fire-
fighters. The immediate issues concern the
manual and non-manual employees. Historically, these occupations have been divided
between a number of unions and a lot of
different arrangements. A process of amalgamation has brought this down to two
unions, one representing manual and non-
manual employees (UNISON) and the other
maintenance workers (the Amalgamated
Engineering and Electrical Union, AEEU).
Relations between management and unions
have been fairly adversarial. The forerunners
of both UNISON and the AEEU were well

organised locally and their members
in London Borough have played
major roles in national disputes
through the years.

The 1997 Framework National Agreement on Harmonisation

In 1997 a new national-level agreement
was reached between the unions and representatives from all the local authorities. As
well as providing for an annual pay increase
and a reduction in the working week, this
was a landmark agreement for local authorities throughout the UK in several respects.
Most important was the agreement to
harmonise the terms and conditions of
employment of the hitherto-separate categories of manual and non-manual
employees. This had been a long-standing
aspiration of manual employees, given
added momentum by the amalgamation of

several unions to form UNISON, and a raft of equality issues, which threatened to cost local authorities a great deal of money. A second notable feature was a move to 'single table bargaining' embracing the two groups. This is where, instead of negotiating separately with each union, all the unions sit down at the same negotiating table with the employer. However, the craft workers retained their separate arrangements for the time being on the understanding that there would eventually be moves to bring them into a single body in the not-too-distant future.

The third feature was the provision for flexibility in the implementation of national agreements. Local authority managers had been pressing for such flexibility for years and had made some progress. In this agreement, however, things were carried a great deal further to embrace the principle of 'subsidiarity'. In other words, there was a (minimum) standard set of arrangements to which local authorities were expected to conform (although they could exceed them if they wanted). Beyond these, however, local authorities were given a great deal of flexibility to reach arrangements of their own. So, for example, it was agreed that working time arrangements and bonus payments should be a matter for local settlement.

Also recommended was a new job evaluation scheme which could be built on at local level. This allowed employers to pay either according to the arrangements or according to some kind of 'spot' rate to suit local conditions. Underpinning the agreement was a statement of principles in which the parties at national level sought to make expressly clear the direction of the relationship they wished to encourage:

The National Joint Council represents local authorities in the United Kingdom and their employees ... We are jointly committed to local democratic control of services to the community as the primary role of local government. Our principal role is to reach agreement, based on shared values, on a national scheme of pay and conditions for local application throughout the UK.

The National Joint Council's (NJC) guiding principles are to support and encourage:

(a) high quality services delivered by a well-trained, motivated workforce with security of employment. To this end, local authorities are encouraged to provide training and development opportunities for their employees;

(b) equal opportunities in employment: equality as a core principle which underpins both service delivery and employment relations; and both the removal of all discrimination and promotion of positive action;

(c) a flexible approach to providing services to the community, which meets the needs of employees as well as employers;

(d) stable industrial relations and negotiation and consultation between local authorities and recognised trade unions.

The NJC has a strong commitment to joint negotiation and consultation at all levels, and to this end encourages employees to join and remain in recognised trade unions. Cooperation between employers, employees and unions will help ensure the successful delivery of services. Local authorities are therefore encouraged to provide facilities to allow trade unions to organise effectively for individual and collective representation. (Statement of principle accompanying 1997 national agreement, unpublished)

Considerable problems were experienced in implementing the 1997 national agreement in London Borough. In particular, there were problems in introducing a reduction in the working week without increasing costs and in implementing the new recommended job evaluation scheme.

The approach from UNISON

The catalyst for a debate over partnership agreements has been the appointment of a new UNISON official who was involved in the negotiation of one of the pioneering partnership agreements involving Welsh Water described above. He has written to the director of personnel services at London Borough suggesting that the management and union should think about making a new beginning. In particular, he has suggested that they seek to put their relationship locally on something like the same basis as the national agreement – in his own words that they should think about introducing a partnership agreement to help them to reach the best standards in management–union relations in the country.

The director of personnel services has asked for some time to think about the initiative. After discussions with senior officers and key figures on the personnel policy committee, a small working party has been formed to consider the response.

CASE ANALYSIS – THE ISSUES

You are asked to address the following questions in the light of the UNISON initiative and the information in the background briefing:

1. Describe the current management style in the London Borough. How far would this have to change for a partnership agreement to be successful? What do you consider to be the major hurdles that have to be dealt with in introducing a partnership agreement and can you see any particular problems in doing so in a local authority?

2. How widespread do you think the applicability of partnership arrangements is? How relevant, for example, do you think such arrangements are to your own organisation?

3. What, in your opinion, would be the major implications of having a partnership agreement for (a) managers and (b) trade unions? Having considered these questions, how would you advise the senior officers to respond to UNISON's proposal to introduce a partnership agreement and why?

4. What sort of benchmarks for assessing the success or failure of a partnership agreement would you recommend be put in place?

REFERENCES

Allen, M. (1998) 'All-inclusive', *People Management*, June, **4**(12): 38–40.

Arrowsmith, J. and Sisson, K. (2000) 'Managing working time' in Bach, S. and Sisson, K. (eds) *Personnel Management: A Comprehensive Guide To Theory and Practice*, 3rd edn. Oxford: Blackwell.

Daniels, K. (1993) 'A comment on Brockner et al.', *Strategic Management Journal*, **16**: 325–8.

Department of Trade and Industry/Department for Education and Employment (1997) *Partnerships with People*. London: DTI.

Edmonds, J. and Tuffin, A. (1990) *A New Agenda*. London: GMB/UCW.

European Foundation for the Improvement in Living and Working Conditions (1997) *New Forms of Work Organisation. Can Europe Realise its Potential? Results of a Survey of Direct Employee Participation in Europe*. Luxembourg: Office for the Official Publications of the European Communities.

European Commission (1997) *Partnership for a New Organisation of Work*. Luxembourg: Office for the Official Publications of the European Communities.

Flood, P. and Toner, B. (1997) 'Large non-union companies: how do they avoid a Catch 22?', *British Journal of Industrial Relations*, **35**: 2.

Greenhalgh, L. and Sutton, R. (1991) 'Organisational effectiveness and job insecurity' in Hartley, J., Jacobson, D., Klandermans, B. and Van Muren, T. (eds) *Job Insecurity, Coping with Jobs at Risk*. London: Sage.

IRS Employment Trends (1992) 'Lean production – and Rover's "New deal"', *Industrial Relations Review and Report*, June, **514**: 12–15.

IRS Employment Trends (1995) 'Employee representation arrangements 1: the trade unions', *IRS Employment Review*, June, **586**: 5–9.

IRS Employment Trends (1997) 'Cementing a new partnership at Blue Circle', *IRS Employment Review*, August, **638**: 5–9.

IRS Employment Trends (1998) 'Partnership in practice at Legal and General', *IRS Employment Review*, February, **650**: 12–16.

Involvement and Participation Association (1992) *Towards Industrial Partnership. A New Approach to Relationships at Work*. London: IPA.

Involvement and Participation Association (1997) *Towards Industrial Partnership. New Ways of Working in British Companies*. London: IPA.

Involvement and Participation Association (1998) *The Partnership Company*. London: IPA.

Kochan, T., Katz, H. and McKersie, R.B. (1986) *The Transformation of American Industrial Relations*. New York: Basic Books.

Marchington, M. and Wilkinson, A. (1996) *Core Personnel and Development*. London: Institute of Personnel and Development.

McCarthy, W.E.J. (1988) *The Future of Industrial Democracy*. Fabian Tract 526. London: Fabian Society.

McLoughlin, I. (1993) 'The non-union firm' in Clark, J. (ed.) *Human Resource Management and Technical Change*. London: Sage.

Purcell, J. (1986) 'Employee relations autonomy within a corporate culture', *Personnel Management*, February.

Sisson, K. (1997) 'The new social challenge and its implications', *The Financial Times Mastering Management*, September, pp. 14–18.

Tailby, S. and Winchester, D. (2000) 'Management and trade unions: towards social partnership?' in Bach, S. and Sisson, K. (eds) *Personnel Management: A Comprehensive Guide To Theory and Practice*, 3rd edn. Oxford: Blackwell.

Thomas, T. and Wallis, B. (1998) 'Dwr Cymru/Welsh water: a case study in partnership' in Sparrow, P. and Marchington, M. (eds) *Human Resource Management: the New Agenda*. London: Financial Times/Pitman.

Torrington, D. and Hall, L. (1998) *Human Resource Management*. London: Prentice Hall.

Trades Union Congress (1997) *Partners for Progress. Next Steps for the New Unionism*. London: TUC.

$\mathcal{C}$HAPTER EIGHT

BANKCO: MANAGERIAL AND ORGANISATIONAL LEARNING

ELENA ANTONACOPOULOU

IN THIS CASE STUDY WE AIM TO:

- EXAMINE the nature of learning within organisations

- CONSIDER how managers learn and what impact organisational processes, such as training and development, have on individuals' learning

- EXAMINE the attempt of one bank to become a 'learning organisation' and the mechanisms employed to facilitate individuals' learning and development.

The discussion begins with a review of the existing literature in relation to individual and organisational learning and concentrates on managerial learning and the main factors which facilitate or inhibit it. The relationship between learning and training is also discussed.

*W*HO LEARNS, THE ORGANISATION OR ITS EMPLOYEES?

The interest in learning within organisations has emerged in recent years with the popularisation of the concept of the 'learning organisation' (Senge, 1990; Garvin, 1993). A key theme underlying this concept is that learning is both a means of responding to the challenge of change and a way of achieving competitiveness. Despite its appeal, there is little agreement about the nature of learning and indeed whether it is possible to claim that organisations do or can learn. Key questions about the nature of learning within organisations remain unanswered. For example, how learning develops within organisations, how it is to be conceptualised and demonstrated and what factors facilitate or inhibit learning within changing organisations, although extensively debated in the literature, remain unresolved.

One of the basic concerns is whether learning at the organisational level is the sum total of individual and group learning or an integral part of organisational functioning regardless of whether individuals learn. Some researchers have argued that organisations can learn (Cyert and March, 1963; Fiol and Lyles, 1985), while others have viewed organisational learning as the collective learning of the individuals which constitute the organisation (Pedler et al., 1991). The lack of agreement about the nature of learning within organisations has led to different propositions about the way learning unfolds and the different types of learning that may be sought. For example, Senge (1990) distinguishes between 'adaptive' and 'generative' learning to emphasise respectively how learning can reactively respond to change or proactively create change. This is similar to the distinction which Argyris and Schön (1978) have drawn between 'single loop' and 'double loop' learning. The former is based on corrective action to overcome a problem, while the latter emphasises the need to question the basic assumptions which have guided the original action and may have caused the problem.

These diverse perspectives confirm that there is a long way to go before agreement can be reached about what learning within organisations is and how it may (or may not) differ from individual learning. It is clear, however, that learning is a human activity. Therefore, it is important to understand how individuals within organisations learn before we can explore whether learning can be examined at other levels of analysis.

HOW DO INDIVIDUALS LEARN?

The way managers construct reality within their organisations depends to a large extent on how and what they learn from the experiences they encounter, and how that learning informs their understanding, perceptions and attitudes towards events. On the basis of adults' distinctive characteristics, namely their roles, responsibilities, life experiences and their overall social development, researchers have proposed several characteristics about the way adults learn. These characteristics are summarised by Jones (1995: 117) and set out in Table 8.1.

The principles of adult learning help us to understand individuals' approaches and potential attitudes towards learning oppor-

Table 8.1 Assumptions about adult learning

- Adults seek autonomy and self-direction
- Adults learn through using their own and others' experience
- Adults want to start learning when they experience a need to know or to do something in order to perform better in some parts of their lives
- Adults tend to be task-oriented or problem-oriented in their approach to learning
- Adults are far more motivated by self-esteem, increased self-confidence, and personal recognition than they are by such things as salary, promotion, status or pay grade

tunities. For example, a unique characteristic of adult learning is that individuals do not approach learning with the straightforward intention of soaking up knowledge. Adults compare a new piece of information with what they already know and test it against their views and prejudices in relation to their own working situation.

These theories have had a significant impact on the development of theory and research in relation to how managers learn within organisations. For example, the recognition that individuals cannot be forced to learn has led to an appreciation that individuals have different learning styles. Thus, research into managers' preferred style of learning (Sutcliffe, 1988) revealed that there are several different types of learner:

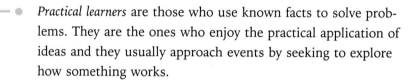

- *Practical learners* are those who use known facts to solve problems. They are the ones who enjoy the practical application of ideas and they usually approach events by seeking to explore how something works.

- *Analytical learners* are more interested in ideas than people. Their strengths lie in creating intellectual concepts, because they examine everything with 'What … ?'

- *Action learners* often learn by trial and error and they examine everything with an 'If … '.

- *Concept learners* are the ones interested in people. They are imaginative and good at listening and sharing ideas, and approach learning by seeking to understand why something happens.

Traditionally management development and training have taken one of two broad forms:

- *On-the-job-training* is precisely that, training that is carried out while the job is being carried out in the normal work situation. This ranges from 'sitting next to Nellie' where the trainee copies the actions of a more experienced operator to more sophisticated methods of coaching and mentoring.

- *Off-the-job-training* includes all training that occurs away from the actual job itself. It includes courses and seminars run by outside organisations and the use of management consultants.

The bulk of managers' learning generally takes place in the workplace, as a result of their work and role activities, in other words, on-the-job learning appears to be the most prevalent and most effective form of learning. It has been argued that, while on-the-job learning is more relevant and useable, much off-the-job formalised learning activity, for example on training courses and seminars, tends to be far removed from the real world of managers. Furthermore, it is claimed that when off-the-job learning does occur, it presents the manager with major difficulties in transferring knowledge back to the work environment (see Casey, 1980).

The recognition that managerial learning consists of unstructured, discontinuous and often unconscious aspects has generated an interest in the experiences that managers encounter and the actions they take. Experiential learning and action learning theories aim to address this issue by placing importance on the social, cultural and political aspects surrounding the learning process. The main characteristics of each of these theories are summarised in Table 8.2.

Table 8.2 Experiential and action learning theories		
	Experiential learning	Action learning
Basic assumptions	Learning follows a four-stage cycle (concrete experience, reflective observation, abstract conceptualisation and active experimentation) which engages the 'whole' person, self-actualisation	Learning by doing, with and from others. Learning involves awareness of one's own values and taking action towards their fulfilment
Orientation to teaching and learning	Learning is a dynamic process involving active participation. Compatibility with individual preferred learning style important	Developing individual's ability to learn – learning to learn – and raising self-awareness and the search for new knowledge

THE FACTORS WHICH INHIBIT OR FACILITATE MANAGERIAL LEARNING

People cannot be forced to learn against their will. The learning process will be most effective when managers themselves recognise a learning need and decide to engage in this process. According to Stewart and Stewart (1981), there are four conditions that facilitate learning:

- the learner must *see a connection* between what she or he takes as the learning task and the potential consequences

- there must be *feedback* on performance if it is to improve

- there must be an *opportunity to practise*, especially when learning a new skill

- *help with a specific skill*, such as vocabulary, can be useful in those areas where people's analytical capabilities are impoverished, for example interpersonal skills.

The capabilities that already exist in the individual before learning begins are also significant in facilitating learning.

Although it is generally perceived that every individual will have some capacity to learn, the context in which learning takes place could determine *what* the individual chooses to learn and *why* (the underlying motive behind learning) as well as *how* the individual is likely to go about learning. A constructive organisational climate encourages individuals to have a positive attitude towards learning and recognise the need to develop learning, to overcome their own resistance to change, to understand their own shortcomings as learners and to be more open to experiences and ready to learn from them. Mumford (1989) provides a list of factors which in his view should be present in any organisation which is said to encourage learning:

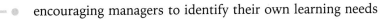

- encouraging managers to identify their own learning needs

- regularly reviewing performance and learning

- encouraging managers to set learning goals for themselves

- providing feedback on both performance and learning

- reviewing managers' performance in developing others

- assisting managers to see learning opportunities on the job

- providing new experiences from which managers can learn

- providing or facilitating the use of training on the job

- tolerating some mistakes

- encouraging the review and planning of learning activities

- challenging the traditional ways of doing things.

Personal and organisational factors can inhibit, as well as facilitate, learning. Stewart and Stewart (1981) propose five factors that will inhibit managers' learning:

- *Learning is a skill* that can be learned but can also be forgotten. Managers that are out of practice, that is, have forgotten or have never acquired learning skills may be found in shock.

- Some *people prefer to be comfortable rather than efficient,* and they may do whatever they can to ensure that nothing interferes with their comfort. Therefore they reject anything that is likely to change their ways or, more significantly, expose or threaten them. Managers may be in a comfort zone in relation to their present level of knowledge and may feel that acquiring additional learning will expose some incompetence.

- Managers are sometimes *'overmotivated' to perform well,* which may inhibit their actual learning (both in terms of quantity and quality) because they aim to achieve too many things at once. This may be the case when pay is strongly related to performance.

- Uncertainty surrounding training and its purpose. Managers attend training, not just to improve performance but for all sorts of reasons. Courses are often used as rewards, punishments and opportunities to keep people busy, while their future is being decided. Such *hidden agendas* inhibit learning and affect managers' perception of the role of training to their development.

- The *role of the trainer*. Not only can their jargon be confusing, they are often concerned not just to train, but to prove that what they teach is the 'one and only' right way of doing things, thus failing to show empathetic understanding towards the needs of the individual which may result in a block to learning.

Organisational structure, culture and communication can also have a significant impact on the learning process and act as organisational barriers to managers' learning. For example, the structure and culture of an organisation may provide a block to learning if they contradict the message provided during formal training sessions. The main obstacles to managers' learning are set out below:

Personal factors

- perception of the need to learn

- perception of the ability to learn

- cultural values and beliefs

- emotional responses

- attitudes towards updating

- intellectual/mental capacity

- age

- memory

- ability to communicate.

Organisational factors

 - internal organisational system of work

- organisational systems, for example training

- culture and climate

- decision-making processes

- communication and feedback

- politics and aversion to risk

- instability and change

- economic position, competition

- power and control.

SUPPORTING LEARNING

Despite the hype of the learning organisation ideal, there is little evidence that organisations are investing in new initiatives to encourage and support learning. For example, organisations do not appear to be prepared to provide training which contributes to the broader development of the individual, or educational opportunities which might encourage employees (including managers) to have more interest in education and learning. The result is an extremely limited range of learning opportunities within organisations and a strong reliance on traditional training programmes to provide learning. Indeed, many organisations have sought to do this even though there is little evidence to support the view that learning is an integral part of the training process or that training provides a good learning opportunity. Furthermore, most organisations seek to use training to enhance learning without even considering that individuals may have different learning styles and different expectations from training interventions (Antonacopoulou, 1999).

In light of this overreliance on training, it is perhaps even more worrying to note that while some organisations do place importance on training, for example Rover spends 6% of its payroll on training, which represents an average of £800 per employee (Mueller, 1991), this picture is by no means universal and many organisations do not appear to take training seriously at all. A number of international comparisons have continued to show that relative to its major competitors the UK has a poor training record (see Constable and McCormick, 1987; Handy, 1987). In an attempt to change attitudes and rectify the situation, successive governments have introduced several initiatives in relation to education and training (for example the Management Charter Initiative, National Vocational Qualifications, Investors in People). These initiatives were intended to highlight the importance of investing in the development of human resources, but, while some studies have shown some increase in both the spending on training and the volume of training undertaken (see Felstead and Green, 1994), there seems to have been little change in fundamental attitudes towards the importance of training and development.

In Chapter 2 it was noted that different systems of corporate ownership and control seen under insider and outsider systems had an important impact on the likelihood of long-term investment in human resources. This and other reasons which may account for the continuing reluctance to spend money on training are as follows:

External factors

- *Emphasis on short-term results within British companies.* Shareholders pressurise companies to maximise short-term returns thus preventing long-term investment in training and development. Companies which have looked to the longer term, such as Lucas, have been punished by the City and have faced takeover threats.

- *The lack of a coherent, and well-funded system of training and vocational education*. The government has continuously tampered with the training framework, introducing measures which have more to do with reducing youth unemployment than improving training provision.

Internal factors

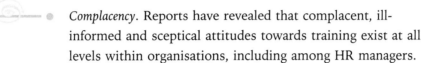

- *Complacency*. Reports have revealed that complacent, ill-informed and sceptical attitudes towards training exist at all levels within organisations, including among HR managers.

- *Weakness of demand for a more highly skilled workforce*. Many UK firms compete on the basis of price, producing standardised and relatively low-cost products. They use a low-paid workforce and have little need for a highly trained workforce.

One important factor in the failure to appreciate the importance of training is the failure to monitor and evaluate training and development activities. In practice, evaluation is difficult to do and, even where organisations attempt it, they rarely use the results of the evaluation exercise to alter training provision. In a survey across ten European countries, the UK came third highest, with 38% of organisations unable to say how much money, as a proportion of wages, was spent on training each year, which contrasted sharply with France where only 2% of organisations did not know (Torrington and Hall, 1998: 411). The failure to monitor and evaluate training and development stems partly from the fact that in any narrow cost–benefit exercise it is much easier to identify the costs of training than to point to clear measurable benefits. There are, however, a number of ways in which this can be done, however imperfectly:

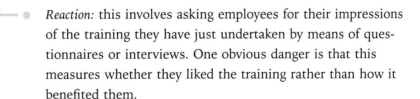

- *Reaction:* this involves asking employees for their impressions of the training they have just undertaken by means of questionnaires or interviews. One obvious danger is that this measures whether they liked the training rather than how it benefited them.

- *Learning:* how well have employees understood the concepts and ideas presented on a training programme? Of course this does not guarantee that the employee can apply the learning on the job.

- *Behaviour:* this measures the impact of training on job behaviour by means of interview and observation. However, even if behaviour changes this may not always yield the results that managers want.

- *Results – 'hard' measures:* the impact of training on the achievement of specified goals can be measured and the position before and after training can be compared. In some jobs this is relatively easy to measure, for example keyboard speed. In others, 'hard' criteria may not be applicable or it may be hard to separate out the impact of training from other influences.

- *Results – 'soft' measures:* the impact of training on recruitment, retention and career management also needs to be evaluated. This is partly due to the interdependency between training and other human resource policies. However, it also reflects the fact that those organisations which apply broader criteria to evaluating their training activity tend to place a higher priority on training. These organisations look beyond training activities to the broader issues of human resource management and organisational effectiveness.

Where organisations attach considerable importance to training, two factors seem to be present. First, what Pettigrew et al. (1988: 28) call the 'business strategic' factor. This refers to the extent to which an organisation's environment is changing, for example technological or product market changes which signal a skills gap or the need to alter the company culture. The second relates to the recognition of the contribution that training can make to an organisation's performance. These factors relate to the politics and personalities of the organisation, the key point being whether there is a positive culture which is supportive of training.

In companies such as ICI, British Steel and Jaguar the importance of training has clearly been viewed as a priority at board level.

DOES TRAINING PROVIDE A LEARNING OPPORTUNITY?

From the point of view of the organisation, learning and training are strongly interconnected, the underlying assumption being that organisations provide training so that individuals will become more competent and, therefore, more effective in their job. From the individual's perspective, a prerequisite for any successful learning opportunity is that the individual is motivated to learn and sees that what is to be learned is relevant to the achievement of his or her personal goals (Gagné, 1970). However, research has demonstrated that the individual's motivation to learn is influenced by a whole range of personal factors (such as career planning and job involvement), situational influences (such as the degree of choice in attending a training programme) and the way in which the work environment is perceived in relation to the constraints and characteristics of the work situation. Moreover, Al-Maskati and Thomas's (1994) study showed that trainees were worried that they might be evaluated while undertaking training and their weaknesses reported back to their superiors via the instructors/trainers of the course, which might have affected their promotion. Such political behaviour is fuelled during performance appraisal reviews which frequently act as the means for identifying training needs as well as the basis for assessing rewards and promotion.

Finally, a significant issue in the relationship between learning and training is the extent to which organisations 'really' want employees to learn. Keep points out that:

Traditional styles of management, based on authoritarian, non-participatory tenets are unlikely to sit easily alongside demands to communicate with and to involve employees ... bearing in mind the education and training of British managers, it is open to question how genuine would be their welcome for a better-educated, better-trained, more self-reliant and questioning workforce. (1989: 123)

THE RETAIL BANKING SECTOR

The retail banking sector provides an interesting example of an industry which has undergone a process of reconstruction which has demanded fast responsiveness to change and a high need for learning. In recent years, competitive pressures have forced retail banks to become more international and global in outlook and to rethink the basics of (retail) banking if they are to survive in the market (Carroll, 1992; McCormick and Rose, 1994). These trends have resulted in noticeable changes in the structure of the industry through mergers, acquisitions and the emergence of new players. This has served to intensify competition and has contributed to the development of new marketing and management techniques.

Training and development have played a key role in creating the stability that the sector has traditionally enjoyed. School-leavers were recruited and trained through a formal, disciplined classroom approach, leading to examinations and professional qualifications (such as the Association of the Chartered Institute of Banking Diploma – ACIBD). However, training and development are also playing a key role in the implementation of the new changes observed in the sector. Investment in training, in order to keep abreast of new developments, is increasingly linked to profitability and is seen as a significant factor in competitive success (Gould, 1988). Recent developments in the sector, however, have shifted the emphasis of management training from technical skills towards management skills, with particular emphasis on sales and marketing (Howcroft, 1989). While formal training is intended to match individuals' speed of learning and assist them up the promotion ladder, informal on-the-job training is also increasingly encouraged as a means of acquiring basic banking skills.

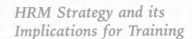

THE CASE STUDY

*B*ANKCO

*A*s a result of changes in the financial services sector, Bankco has undergone numerous operational and strategic changes over the past few years. One of the most significant changes has been the cultural shift from being operational to becoming more sales oriented. Bankco was restructured from 7 regions and 54 districts, to 3 regions and 21 areas. Customer services centres have been established and have begun to take a large part of the administrative work out of the branches. This shift has been reflected in the redesign of Bankco's premises and in particular the branch network and the technology for delivering services. These changes have resulted in a substantial reduction of staff, over 9,000 since 1989. The composition of staff has also changed dramatically. Bankco lost many of its older and more experienced managers and became a 'younger' organisation (most managers now are in their mid-thirties). Nearly 400 branches were closed down during the period 1990–95. These changes have led to a reconsideration of training and development policies and practices and a greater emphasis on learner-centred approaches.

HRM Strategy and its Implications for Training

Bankco's HRM strategy aims to secure:

*S*killed, motivated and professional staff. We recognise that staff are our key resource and have the power to differentiate us from the competition in the minds of our customers. (training manager)

The HRM function in Bankco is organised in four main units: human resource planning; training and development; employee relations; and personnel operation. Training, in particular, has been seen as a central platform for implementing the HRM strategy both historically and currently. One of the traditional practices in this and other organisations in the sector has been to use training to support change programmes. In other words, training is seen as a key communication tool and a means of providing staff with the necessary knowledge and skills to respond to the new requirements.

According to training providers, the commitment of Bankco to supporting staff development is demonstrated by the substantial investment in training, particularly during the difficult days of the economic recession in the early 1990s. The training budget during 1993 was £17 million, an increase on previous years. Approximately 25,000 training days were allocated during the same year. Moreover in 1993 approximately 5,600 managers had gone through a training programme in one of Bankco's staff colleges. The structure of the training and development (T&D) department is fairly flat and consists of five main units; namely resourcing and development, HR quality, training design and delivery, equal opportunities and residential training. The department is responsible for the design and coordination of training programmes both centrally and locally (at the regional level).

The training and development policy states that the purpose of Bankco's training and development investment is:

*t*o ensure that we have an appropriately skilled, highly motivated and professional staff who deliver consistently to required national standards. To do this we ensure that: each individual understands exactly what their job requires; each individual is trained to perform their current job to required standards; staff are prepared for future challenges created by the business; and each individual is enabled to develop his/her potential.

An Emphasis on Learning

A unique feature of the training process within Bankco is the emphasis placed on learning. This is a recent (1992) change in training orientation which resulted from a survey which suggested that 60% of Bankco's employees felt that 'training and learning [meant] attending courses'. These results encouraged Bankco to reconsider its training methods (such as computer-based training, residential and non-residential courses, seminars, interactive video and so on) and to introduce a wider range of flexible approaches (for example self-development and self-directed learning, learning resource centres) which enable managers to have access to learning material and packages (books, video tapes, audio tapes, self-study packages and work-based learning activities such as coaching, job shadowing, job rotation, secondments, project work). The shift to more flexible training methods was intended to encourage staff at all levels to explore other learning opportunities and not rely on training courses alone in order to learn. The new training policy explains that:

*l*earning is not just about going on courses, it is about consciously using your work activities to develop yourself. Making the most of other support and learning resources now available. Taking responsibility for your own learning means you will be able to fulfil your development needs.

This new training policy, which reflected a major cultural change effort, was driven by the HR department, which had considerable power. Bankco embraced the notion of the learning organisation in the belief that becoming a learning organisation would enable it to remain competitive and successful in the light of the current upheaval in the sector. This led to a series of initiatives intended to encourage staff at all levels to take responsibility for their own learning and to encourage them to seek to learn from diverse sources.

The Transition to a Learning Organisation

The new initiatives were intended to support Bankco's objective 'to move away from a *push* strategy towards a *pull* strategy' (HR manager). In other words, instead of sending people on training courses because their line manager believed they needed it, the individual would actively seek to further his or her own development and would take responsibility for this. In the words of a senior training manager: 'The challenge for us is to move to a situation where it is not the business training the staff, but it is the business providing opportunities within which the staff can learn and grow.' The recent changes in training philosophy within Bankco have sought to create a partnership between the individual, the line manager and the T&D department. The training policy states explicitly that:

*t*he responsibility of line managers is to guide individuals in how best to equip themselves for their current and future roles. They are also responsible for ensuring that appropriate action takes place. The prime responsibility for learning rests with individuals in partnership with their line manager.

The aim in introducing self-development is not purely improvement of financial performance, but a concern with changing individual attitudes towards training and learning. The transition is recognised by training managers as a cultural change for the bank, because 'managers are not used to taking responsibility for their self-development' (training manager).

One of the mechanisms adopted to assist this transition is the 'continuous learning' project. The project aims to develop a package of audiovisual aids, as well as a booklet guiding managers and staff on how to utilise the various learning opportunities that are available to them. A key feature of this process is the introduction of personal development plans (PDPs) and specialist development programmes designed to cultivate responsibility for self-development at all levels.

The Managers' Perspective

It was clear from the interviews with managers in Bankco that, in relation to learning as a process, they perceived that people learn primarily as a result of on-the-job experiences, modelling or copying others and traditional teaching through training. A significant proportion of managers (62%) suggested that practical, on-the-job experiences were the most significant, because they provided 'hands-on learning', 'coming across new situations and acting upon them'. These managers believed that an experience provides learning when managers try to do something themselves. In the words of one manager this would involve 'putting theory into practice and seeing how you can expand on it'.

Managers also believed that experience in a social context was important and suggested that discussion with others was an important learning experience. Observing, listening and copying were important activities in the learning process. Managers taking this view of learning recognised the influence of other managers, particularly line managers.

Finally, managers in Bankco perceived that learning took place in formal teaching environments, most commonly on training courses. Managers who took this view maintained the attitude derived from their school years, namely that learning is about 'being taught'. One manager supporting this view pointed out that: 'people learn because they are told to. People do not often take the initiative.' Some managers recognised that organisational structures and systems may

have forced people to develop similar learning patterns. One manager made the following comment:

Individuals learn very much in the same way; by absorbing information, by making it interesting, relating it to real life situations. Absorption involves recollection, using key words, revision, competition and reward in the end.

Other factors had helped to shape managers' views. Managers identified a combination of personal and organisational factors. At the personal level, managers gave particular emphasis to the individual's 'willingness and desire to learn' and 'the commitment to improving one's self'. At the organisational level a significant proportion of managers (42%) felt that the organisational context made all the difference to managerial learning. As one manager put it, 'it's the learning environment whereby people are encouraged to challenge and be creative'. The organisation was perceived to 'provide the resources and the space for learning' and 'to set the boundaries and the standards that individuals need to follow'. Therefore, the organisational context 'channels ability into the direction which is in line with organisational needs'.

Training was also felt to have a significant influence. Managers referred specifically to 'participative training methods where everyone can have an input and can gain a broad perspective'. A significant proportion (58%) referred to a specific internal training course as their ideal learning experience. Training courses were seen in this way when they 'employ[ed] a variety of learning methods' and 'enabled managers to relate the knowledge acquired to real life'. The use of a variety of learning methods was also felt to facilitate the 'development of a team spirit' and 'encourages participants to share experiences with other participants and to learn from each other'. Managers taking this view claimed that training courses are a 'back to school' experience, because they enable managers to 'dedicate time to education without being interrupted'.

A large proportion (77%) of the managers in Bankco supported a strong connection between learning and training, primarily because they considered training as an opportunity for learning, for them training and learning were 'one and the same thing'. Managers described this strong association by saying: 'obviously training and learning are related. The very word training implies that you will learn from the process'. Another manager added that: 'it is a specific time to learn, you know you are there to learn'. The fact that you are taken away from the work environment was seen by some managers as a factor enabling them to be in the 'right frame of mind for learning'.

However, despite the close association between training and learning, it is impor-tant to note that training was also perceived by some managers to be one of the main obstacles to their learning. For example, managers perceived that there was no link between training and future career development 'the higher up the organisation one gets, the less assistance is provided. The assumption is that once you reach a certain position you know it all.' Moreover, managers felt that they '[did] not have the necessary power or control' over their learning. In addition, a 'limited recognition for learning' was an added source of 'demotivation' and 'reduces willingness to learn'.

Evaluating Training and Learning

Bankco had not yet systematically evaluated the success of the PDP initiative, partly because it was new and partly because there was no systematic evaluation of training provision generally within the organisation. In practice PDPs are used to monitor managers' self-development activities, having been introduced as part of the performance appraisal review. The performance appraisal remained the main mechanism for identifying individuals' training needs. One training manager made the following remarks:

The biggest barrier at the moment is that they say the individual takes responsibility and the individual drives the responsibility, but the pace of change is so great that the poor individual doesn't have any time at all to do it and the pressure's certainly that in saying to the individual it is your responsibility to plan your learning and come up with suggestions about what you should do ... it's a good idea but it just isn't working ... We have a performance management system and this system is very sophisticated and there are nine sections that people's performance in managerial practices are rated. The least valued section is self-development. So what this is saying is that if your performance on self-development is rated good and your performance against the other managerial practices is rated medium, then you will come out as medium overall. That's how we demonstrated a year ago that self-development was the least valued of the managerial practices.

A large proportion of managers within Bankco felt that the organisation encouraged them to learn (54%) and to develop themselves (73%). This would suggest that the emphasis placed by Bankco on learning and self-development is acknowledged by managers. According to managers, the use of PDPs indicates the organisation's encouragement for learning and self-development. Managers explained that because PDPs have been introduced by the organisation, they are seen to be a positive indication that the organisation will hold individuals responsible for their self-development. Managers

explained that 'self-development had been a major theme over the last couple of years', as evident through 'the company's magazine', 'internal circulars', 'conferences' and 'team meetings'.

On closer examination, however, when managers considered the implications of the organisation's encouragement for learning and for self-development in practice, they interpreted this as an 'expectation'. In other words, managers felt that 'the organisation expected [them] to learn, to remain up to date and to be able to respond positively to the new requirements set upon [them]'. Moreover, this view derived from the association of self-development with performance appraisal. Managers explained that during the performance appraisal process they had to demonstrate that they recognised their strengths and weaknesses and were clear about what they needed to do in order to improve themselves. One manager made the following remarks: 'In the performance management system, individuals are asked to identify personal development initiatives. In some respects it forces you to think of something.' Another manager explained that because of the link between self-development and performance appraisal: 'you have to show you do something, otherwise you are scored low and your salary is affected'. A senior manager said: 'you're not encouraged, you're expected to. You're expected to know things ... you do it for your own protection.'

These views show quite clearly that not only do managers believe that there is an expectation for them to learn new things (rather than merely an encouragement) but that the organisation's approach has also affected their interpretation of what learning and self-development mean and how they should go about them. This helps to explain why managers may be limiting themselves to learning and developing primarily from the resources provided within organisational settings. Moreover, it helps to explain why managers rely on training in order to learn. The views of the managers interviewed clearly support Bankco's survey results regarding attitudes towards learning and training, and show that despite the attempt to change staff attitudes, managers appear to hold exactly the same view that they did before the new initiatives, that is, that learning and training are the same thing.

CASE ANALYSIS – THE ISSUES

In analysing the case you are asked to address the following issues:

1. Evaluate Bankco's objective of becoming a learning organisation in light of its business and HRM strategies.

2. Consider to what extent Bankco is laying the foundations for becoming a learning organisation. How far do you think Bankco has been successful in its objectives? What are the main challenges it has encountered so far?

3. Recommend an action plan on issues, activities and changes that this bank would need to introduce in order to facilitate or enhance managerial learning.

4. Analyse the role of the HR function in Bankco. How might the HR function assist or impede the implementation of your action plan?

REFERENCES

Al-Maskati, H. and Thomas, A.B. (1994) *Why Managers Don't Learn*. Paper presented at the British Academy of Management Conference, Lancaster.

Antonacopoulou, E.P. (1999) 'Training does not imply learning: the individual's perspective', *International Journal of Training and Development*, **3**(1): 27–36.

Argyris, C. and Schön, D.A. (1978) *Organisational Learning: A Theory In Action Perspective*. Reading, MA: Addison Wesley.

Carroll, P. (1992) 'The fallacy of customer retention – the truth of customer retention', *Journal of Retail Banking*, **13**(4): 15–25.

Casey, D. (1980) 'Transfer of learning – there are two separate problems' in Beck, J.E. and Cox, C.J. (eds) *Advances in Management Education*. Chichester: John Wiley.

Constable, J. and McCormick, R. (1987) *The Making Of Managers*. A report for BIM and CBI into management training, education and development. London: BIM.

Cyert, R.M. and March, J.G. (1963) *A Behavioural Theory of The Firm*. Englewood Cliffs, NJ: Prentice Hall.

Felstead, A. and Green, F. (1994) 'Cycles of training? Evidence from the British recession of the early 1990s' in Booth, A. and Snower, D. (eds) *The Skills Gap And Economic Activity*. Cambridge: Cambridge University Press.

Fiol, C.M. and Lyles, M.A. (1985) 'Organisational learning', *Academy of Management Review*, **10**(4): 803–13.

Gagné, R.M. (1970) *The Conditions Of Learning*. New York: Holt, Reinhart & Winston.

Garvin, D.A. (1993) 'Building a learning organisation', *Harvard Business Review*, July–August, pp. 78–91.

Gould, D. (1988) 'Doing what comes unnaturally', *The Banker*, **138**(744): 60–6.

Handy, C. (1987) 'Management training: perk or prerequisite?', *Personnel Management*, May.

Howcroft, J.B. (1989) 'Retail branch banking, issues in the United Kingdom', *Journal of Retail Banking*, **11**(1): 11–17.

Jones, A.M. (1995) 'A learning in organisations model' in Bradshaw, D.C.A. (ed.) *Bringing Learning To Life: The Learning Revolution, The Economy and The Individual*. London: Falmer Press.

Keep, E. (1989) 'Corporate training strategies: the vital component?' in Storey, J. (ed.) *New Perspectives On Human Resource Management*. London: Routledge.

McCormick, J.M. and Rose, S. (1994) 'Restoring relevance to retail banking', *Journal of Retail Banking*, **16**(1): 5–10.

Mumford, A. (1989) *Management Development – Strategies for Action*. London: Institute of Personnel Management.

Mueller, F. (1991), 'A new engine of change in employee relations', *Personnel Management*, July.

Pedler, M., Burgoyne, J. and Boydell, T. (1991) *The Learning Company*. London: McGraw-Hill.

Pettigrew, A., Sparrow, P. and Hendry, C. (1988) 'The forces that trigger training', *Personnel Management*, December.

Senge, P.M. (1990) 'The leaders' new work: building learning organisations', *Sloan Management Review*, Fall, pp. 7–23.

Stewart, V. and Stewart, A. (1981) *Tomorrow's Managers Today*, 2nd edn. London: Institute of Personnel Management.

Sutcliffe, G.E. (1988) *Effective Learning For Effective Management*. London: Prentice Hall.

Torrington, D. and Hall, L. (1998) *Human Resource Management*. London: Prentice Hall.

CHAPTER NINE

PHARMACO: ORGANISATIONAL RESTRUCTURING AND JOB INSECURITY

HELEN NEWELL AND CAROLINE LLOYD

IN THIS CASE STUDY WE AIM TO:

- EXAMINE the way in which job insecurity was managed in the aftermath of redundancy and takeover in the manufacturing division of a pharmaceutical company

- EXPLORE the extent to which a company felt it necessary to take steps to manage feelings of job insecurity among different groups of employees.

JOB INSECURITY

Job insecurity is an increasingly important feature of employment. As Turnbull and Wass (2000: 57) report:

When asked about the security of their employment the majority of British workers report fears of impending job loss and feelings of insecurity.

They argue that even though academic research on job tenure and turnover appears to indicate that these fears are not justified, other factors do suggest that workers' fear of redundancy is well founded. They point to a significant rise in involuntary job losses, both in absolute terms and as a proportion of all job losses, and the permissiveness of the UK redundancy laws as key influences on workers' views about their job security.

The law confers the right of management to declare redundancies, and provided the employer can demonstrate that any redundancies meet the 'needs of the business' they are unlikely to be challenged by industrial tribunals. (Turnbull and Wass, 2000: 58)

Job insecurity often results from changes in the organisational or economic context, such as mergers or takeovers, which frequently lead to large-scale redundancy programmes. It is not only those employees who lose their jobs through redundancy that experience job insecurity. Those who remain, the 'survivors', often experience changes in their beliefs about the security of their jobs, induced by the feeling that they are 'next in line'. The outcome of this job insecurity can have serious consequences, not only for the individual, but also for organisational effectiveness. While some authors argue that the low esteem and high levels of worry experienced by survivors of redundancy can lead to greater motivation (Brockner et al., 1991), others are less optimistic, arguing that job insecurity can lead to employees being less willing to accept change, more resentful of imposed change and more secretive and competitive (Greenhalgh and Sutton, 1991). Indeed, Daniels (1993) warns that prolonged worry over the threat of future lay-offs may lead to depression, poorer work performance, absenteeism, alcoholism, and drug abuse as well as reducing motivation. Anxiety about future lay-offs may merely elicit inappropriate behaviour from individuals as employees work longer hours in order to be seen to be 'working hard' without necessarily being more effective (Clark, 1994).

THE PSYCHOLOGICAL CONTRACT

One way of understanding the impact of changes in beliefs about job security on the individual is through the concept of the psychological contract. The psychological contract

*d*efines what employees are prepared to give by way of effort and contribution in exchange for something that they value from their employer, such as job security.

(Newell and Dopson, 1996: 4)

Violation of this contract, for example through the withdrawal of job security, has been shown to lead to increased turnover rates, lower levels of trust between employees and managers, less job satisfaction and a growth in the number of employees intending to leave the company (Robinson and Rousseau, 1994). While an intention to leave may not be turned into action, because of the lack of attractive alternatives (Dopson et al., 1997), an employee who wishes to quit, but is constrained from leaving, will alter his or her level of contribution to the organisation. It is not surprising, then, that, in terms of organisational effectiveness and efficiency, research suggests that job insecurity can lead to employees having lower levels of commitment, being less willing to accept change, more resentful of imposed change and more secretive and competitive (Greenhalgh and Sutton, 1991). Despite these potential impacts of restructuring, research shows that most organisations take no steps to evaluate the impact of redundancies on their employees.

EMPLOYEE INVOLVEMENT

Guest and Peccei highlight the importance of 'survivor guilt' among those who remain after redundancy programmes. They argue that if the organisation's employee involvement processes ignore the survivors, 'who may feel more coercion and even less control than those made redundant' (1992: 37), then they are likely to evaluate the whole process more negatively, which in turn will have an impact on the extent to which managers are successful in their goal of enhancing employee commitment to the organisation. They also stress the importance of information and communication processes in shaping survivors' perceptions, and the role of trade unions in this process. Again we see that involving employees in organisational decision-making is a fundamental prerequisite to the successful adoption of human resource policies.

MANAGING INSECURITY

In an attempt to overcome some of these difficulties, Greenhalgh (1991) suggests three types of coping strategies that companies might employ to help manage job insecurity: *preventative, ameliorative* and *restorative. Preventative* strategies aim to preclude insecurity by keeping the workforce basically intact. In practical terms this means finding alternative ways to reduce costs, for example by relying on natural attrition, terminating short-term or temporary contracts, or by organising intra-organisational transfers. The important consideration here is for companies to take into account the total costs of job loss over the long term, including lower productivity, resistance to change, loss of valued survivors (who management intended to retain) and subsequent difficulty in hiring high-quality workers, as well as the possibility of increased rates of grievances and union opposition. However, Greenhalgh acknowledges that many companies will not have the funds available to pursue these strategies, even if they wanted to. Indeed, 'where organisational death is inevitable then long-run economic costs are irrelevant' (1991: 188).

Ameliorative strategies are aimed at minimising the hardships experienced by both job losers and survivors. There are factors within management's discretion which can limit the damage caused by reducing the intensity of job insecurity. For example, the amount of notice displaced workers receive, the way in which job losses are grouped (a single cut rather than waves of smaller cuts), re-employment assistance, continuation of employer support and so on. Greenhalgh argues that the single cut strategy is 'the only way to cut a workforce if the job insecurity of survivors is to be kept within manageable bounds' (1991: 191). Furthermore, since survivors are observing the process, the provision of continued health insurance, severance pay and no loss of pension benefits for redundant workers will all go some way to reducing the survivors' perceptions of the magnitude of the loss suffered and therefore their own potential loss if they are next in line. The message this sends to survivors is that they need not fear total economic loss with no assistance from the organisation, which helps to head off a job insecurity crisis.

Restorative strategies are intended to repair the damage done to the commitment and morale of survivors. These strategies focus specifically on the survivors once the workforce reduction has been completed and ideally involve giving guarantees that there will be no further job losses. However, managers need to be honest in their assurances since false assurances will only help in the short term. The least believable assurance is where managers urge workers not to worry about redundancy because no further job losses are planned. Clearly, the fact that no job losses are currently planned for the future will be of little comfort if it was inadequate planning that led to the previous job loss situation. Furthermore, where assurances are given by personnel managers who do not participate in the strategic planning that will determine future workforce requirements, then such assurances will inevitably lack credibility. Indeed, whoever delivers the assurance, workers tend not to believe managers' good intentions alone. As Greenhalgh comments:

good intentions typically are formed in the aftermath of a job-loss debacle, but the future decision will be made under severe stress, and in the face of powerful new economic pressures. The temptation to settle for expedient short-term solutions will once again become immensely attractive, and the good intentions become overwhelmed. (1991: 196)

However, Greenhalgh does assume that (apart from those facing imminent 'death') all companies will in some way seek to lessen the impact of redundancy and restructuring, and alleviate feelings of insecurity. How likely is it that this will happen in practice? In Chapter 2 we considered the importance of the way in which HRM strategy supports the organisation's business strategy and the extent to which HRM policies are mutually supportive. While we might expect that an organisation pursuing an innovation strategy, with a strong internal labour market and policies associated with a sophisticated HRM style, might be concerned with reducing the impact of job insecurity and building strong employee commitment, can we assume that the same will be true for all organisations in all circumstances?

Greenhalgh noted that in practical terms adopting preventative strategies means finding alternative ways to reduce costs which requires companies to focus on long-term financial consequences. However, we also saw in Chapter 2 that the existence of what can be termed an internal capital market and its accompanying financial control systems within multidivisional companies plays an important role in influencing, if not determining, HRM policy. The use of budgetary control systems with monthly reporting and internal capital markets inevitably forces a short-term financial approach. This leads not only to a short-term cost focus, but also means that there is perceived to be very little control at site level. In a company with strong financial controls and internal competition between sites, should we expect to see the adoption of strategies to cope with job insecurity?

THE PHARMACEUTICAL INDUSTRY

You should refer to the description of the pharmaceutical industry which is provided in Chapter 6. It is often highlighted as one of the few examples of British manufacturing success in high value added markets, with leading-edge technology.

However, recent mergers and takeovers have had a significant impact on the industry in terms of redundancies and site closures. In an industry where the psychological contract between employer and employee has typically been based on loyalty and commitment to the organisation in exchange for employment security and high wages, this has meant a dramatic change for some groups of employees in particular. Most of the research published about pharmaceutical companies focuses on employees engaged in research and development. It is important for the purposes of this case study to appreciate the range of employees and types of job that exist within pharmaceutical companies.

THE CASE STUDY

PHARMACO

Pharmaco was originally part of a large British pharmaceutical and chemical company which, as a result of strong competitive pressures in the 1990s, undertook a major organisational change programme. This led to a number of divisions and plants being sold off, plant closures and hundreds of job losses. The remains of the company were taken over in a hostile bid in 1995 by a large foreign-owned pharmaceutical multinational (Drugco) which closed one of the two sites and transferred product development from the closing site to the remaining site. In the 18 months following the takeover £18m was invested in Pharmaco.

Following the takeover there were some 950 people employed on the site, including 100 employees in chemical operations (manufacture of the basic constituents of the drugs), 300 employees in pharmaceutical operations (manufacturing and packaging processes), 100 employees in industrialisation (where new ideas were developed to an initial production stage) and 122 people in quality control. The rest were split between materials management and warehousing. Approximately 300 of the employees are union members.

Within chemicals there was a considerable degree of uncertainty about how activities would develop in the future. With the loss of patent protection for one of the company's leading drugs and increased competition from producers of generic drugs, discussion had been underway for some time as to whether or not to complete all the process themselves or buy some of it in from elsewhere. A new chemical facility was being built on the site and when it was completed several changes to traditional job organisation were envisaged, particularly in relation to the role of shift manager which was to be replaced by that of 'enhanced team leader' who would report directly to the plant manager.

In the pharmaceuticals area a new state-of-the-art production facility with 'high-speed' filling and packing lines had been installed. Originally it had been announced that only the 'best and most effective people' would move to the new facility and that people would have to apply for their own jobs, but with the arrival of the new director of pharmaceutical operations (following the takeover) a decision was taken to transfer as many of the existing staff as possible to the new facility. The new pharmaceutical facility, like the new chemical facility, was likely to utilise new methods of work organisation.

The Redundancies

The redundancies took place as part of the change programme undertaken by the British parent of Pharmaco 12 months prior to the hostile takeover. The company had employed a well-known consultancy firm to advise them on restructuring. As a result of this exercise a decision was taken to reduce the workforce by 250.

The director of chemical operations believed that the process had been 'managed very well locally, with voluntary redundancies and natural wastage. There were no compulsory redundancies', although he did acknowledge that it was something that was done to the workforce, rather than with them and that lessons ought to be learned from that:

Before Drugco took over there was downsizing on this site – no one was made compulsorily redundant. You could volunteer and quite a lot who were over 50 could take the redundancy and the pension. A small group of staff were told their jobs were at risk. Most found positions elsewhere on the site. Most people were under threat of the axe for some months. No one was thrown out. (shift manager, chemicals)

One of the trade union representatives agreed that in theory there were no compulsory redundancies, but in practice he believed that 'if you were 50 years old you had no choice, you had to go'.

Some areas of the company were more heavily hit by the redundancy programme than others, which appears to have affected views about future job security. In industrialisation there were no redundancies and views about the likelihood of future redundancies were different from those in pharmaceuticals and chemicals. Compare the following comments from employees in different areas of the company:

*M*orale is fine – people aren't gnashing their teeth, things are reasonably buoyant. The whole site and industry have been through a period of concern with [the old company] and restructuring. We were the only department who didn't have the chopper descend on us. Its got to be good. (section manager, industrialisation)

I don't think employment here is safe or secure. The business plan gives you the overall plan, but I've got mixed feelings about what will happen in the next two years. In the past, with half the size, we've had double the levels of production we have now. Something needs to happen. (supervisor, pharmaceuticals)

*I*f they get the new facility going this one will be wound down … the old one is labour intensive, the new one isn't. The future of the department is grim. (operator, chemicals)

The Takeover

Drugco was a typical multidivisional organisation with a corporate headquarters responsible for business policy and planning and the allocation of resources. Not only profits, but also the right to develop and produce new products would be subject to a system of divisional bidding, with corporate management deciding on the allocation between competing divisions. In addition, an extensive set of controls was established which sought to regulate and monitor divisional behaviour. The finance manager in chemicals commented on the 'extreme amount of detail' that corporate head office required, particularly in relation to headcount which he believed was the 'key ratio':

output per head, profit per head, sales per head were all viewed as extremely important. As he put it, 'there's very tight control, you have to show good reasons for an increase and explain away any decrease – if you've done it they want to know how other plants can do it'.

The other driving factor was the need to cut costs. 'The company, site, local management are all regularly prodded or briefed that they have a duty to find ways to do things better, cheaper, more economically. Its part of the budget process. We're asked to reduce costs by £4m in efficiency savings.' Despite the injection of £18m, the general manager also commented on the increased level of competitiveness within the company. He explained that a competitive element had been built in through various performance indicators which 'stack one site up against another'. He described it as a 'finance-driven company – in order to be retained as a key strategic site you have to be successful, to improve utilisation of resources and obtain a good return on investment'. Not only was there competition for resources, but more particularly the competition between the company's 55 manufacturing sites to manufacture new products was severe, as many of them already had spare capacity.

In other ways, however, there was little evidence of a hostile takeover. As the director of chemical operations explained: 'we did not see a whole lot of [new] people march on site and decide to downsize. The site management team were the main casualties.'

Managing Insecurity?

Management expressed frustration that workers failed to see the importance of change and focused instead on the day-to-day detail of their jobs. They wanted employees to take an active part in the running of the business, particularly through the site consultative council (SCC) and were looking for significant operational improvements through direct employee participation and self-managed teams. Employees, they complained, did not seem interested. Management believed that this stemmed from the fact that employees blamed the new company for past job losses and current uncertainties. However, despite this apparent lack of employee interest, very few steps were taken to reduce feelings of continuing job insecurity. One way in which Pharmaco did seek to manage insecurity was through the use of temporary workers as a buffer for permanent staff. As one middle manager in pharmaceuticals commented:

*W*e realise that there are opportunities from moving across [to the new facility] for the head count to be reduced, so as people are leaving we are deliberately replacing them with temps to keep the permanent employees at a manageable level. It's an attempt to minimise repercussions. The temps are employed for variable periods, they have a direct contract with [the company]. We used to be heavily dependent upon agencies, but we tend to move away from that now.

Although management claimed to be using temporary workers to minimise potential job losses, employees in pharmaceuticals were still concerned about the impact that the working arrangements in the new facility, with its high-speed lines, would have on their jobs:

I don't feel that our jobs are secure – the things that people have said – running new high-speed lines will mean job losses and cutting numbers. (operator, pharmaceuticals)

*A*t the business plan briefing they said that we were getting 100% out now, in three years we need to get 150% out. The only way we'll get 150% out is to reduce the headcount. Its only by less people doing the same amount of work. Another year or so and we'll see some more redundancies … workload has halved, why? [The drug] is a 30-year-old product, but two years ago there were two shifts working flat out – so what's happened in the last two years? (operator, pharmaceuticals)

Nor was the use of temporary employees particularly welcomed by either operators or supervisors on the site:

*M*y feeling is that most companies are using a strong temporary workforce. It is easier to manage, cheaper, but it is wrong. I totally disagree with it. The most important thing is job security, more important than earnings and conditions. They have always used a lot of temps in filling but it is new in chems. (operator, chemicals)

*D*espite the temporary staff, people at the moment feel very insecure. If they only want one shift to move over [to the new factory] will they ask me to move over or will they sack us altogether? (operator, pharmaceuticals)

*T*here are a large number of temps – its very frustrating, it messes people's lives up. We are often wasting a lot of time and effort in training people up, I have a lot of sympathy with the temps … I think it's bad employment practice, immoral, despite the pay. There's no pension, how do you keep a mortgage and so on. (supervisor, pharmaceuticals)

For some employees, transfers between areas across the site were seen as possible, particularly in industrialisation where career paths often developed in this way. Outside this relatively privileged area, however, transfers were less common. This was partly because transfers were associated with promotion and it was generally felt that to be promoted you needed a degree qualification, and partly because the mechanism for transfer was to apply for jobs which were advertised on the notice board. Popular job adverts were often quickly removed from the notice board by potential applicants so that other operators would not see them.

With the takeover and the injection of substantial extra money into the site it is tempting to assume that this would have provided the perfect platform for credible reassurances about future job losses and indeed, a minority of employees, particularly in industrialisation, saw the takeover as a source of relief, believing that being part of a bigger company provided better longer term security:

We had lived under a cloud for a long time – not knowing what the future would bring – so Drugco alleviated that, especially when it started to invest in the site, so that side has gone. (technologist, industrialisation)

I'm very encouraged by the prospects, now they've moved R&D up here and they've invested right, left and centre. I think it's a very exciting time. Jobs are now quite secure, well they're never 100% secure are they! (technologist, industrialisation)

However, outside industrialisation, interviewees commented that despite their expectations there had been little to engender greater confidence in the company, especially since the management team had not changed substantially following the takeover. From their point of view only the director of pharmaceutical operations (who came from the new parent company) and the human resources director were seen to be 'new'.

There are a lot of the same people, same positions as [in the old company], there have been reshuffles, but it's a lot of the same old faces. (operator, chemicals)

As a result, in so far as the redundancy programme was seen to result from poor management, not changing the management team was seen to be a significant failing. In other ways, too, little seemed to have changed since the takeover:

They've painted everything a darker shade of blue, that must have cost lots of money! (supervisor, pharmaceuticals)

No difference since Drugco took over. We hoped there would be a shake-up, but all the managers are still the same. They rationalised, cut back managers, now the numbers are right back up again. I don't know what's going on. (operator, chemicals)

The takeover hasn't made any difference. I really thought it would. We've got lots of stock in the basement, We're not filling now, we've done the last orders – so the running of the place is the same as it was. (operator, pharmaceuticals)

Another point of contention was the use of the same consultancy firm that had masterminded the redundancy programme to help devise the new business plan for the site:

… [The consultancy firm] was one of the biggest mistakes they've ever made. Last time they came in there were 400 redundancies, now they've had them back again. (engineer, chemicals and union representative)

But perhaps the most important factor in the managers' inability to reassure employees about the future stability of the site was the failure to develop meaningful employee communication and involvement processes. According to interviewees, employees wanted to be consulted and involved in the changes that were taking place, but they felt that they had little influence over managerial decision-making on a site-wide basis. At the local level, while there was generally felt to be good communications between employees and their line managers, there was a general concern about poor communications with

more senior management. At site level, while there were high levels of union membership in both chemicals and pharmaceuticals, all but one union member felt that the union either lacked strength or had little influence over management:

The unions aren't very strong here, there is very little communications through the company … There is very little consultation. It is a take it or leave it attitude. (operator, chemicals)

There's no understanding that the union could have a real role in helping to run the factory. (engineer)

You go to meetings and battle but come out with nothing … Management listen but they do what they like. It wears people down. Morale is low since the redundancies and it is no better since then. (ex-union representative, pharmaceuticals)

The unions' lack of power meant that the employee voice was not effectively represented, heard or acted on by management. This undermined the credibility of management since it failed to ensure that managers had to explain or justify their decisions. There was a lack of formal mechanisms to involve unions at both site and local levels which ensured that the existing representation structure was not being used to obtain the views of employees on a regular basis. Although there was a staff consultative committee (SCC), employees who were representatives were generally critical of the way in which it was organised, the lack of employee consultation and the lack of management's willingness to consult. In general it was thought to lack any real power as a consultative body and it lacked relevance to employees. Thus the SCC did not provide an alternative forum for the representation of the employees' views. The issues it raised and the way in which this was done did not encourage employee involvement. In all three areas of the plant there was concern over the failure to involve employees either through trade unions or individually in decision-making about changes in work organisation:

There is a recognition that we should involve people and that we haven't done it very well ... There are a lot of barriers to doing that. The environment is never ideal because of the undercapacity. The future is somewhat uncertain in terms of people we need, everybody has got the axe hanging over them ... It demotivates people a bit, there is a reluctance to give fully when they might be out on their ear. (shift manager, chemicals)

When we have meetings lots of points are brought up and it ends up a waste of time.

Nothing is going to happen, it either takes months or it is forgotten about or it is never changed at all. (operator, pharmaceuticals)

Much of the worry and concern about job security stemmed from a perceived lack of information about what was going to happen on the site, from conflicting messages about what would happen in the future, or because employees simply did not believe what they were being told. Indeed some interviewees expressed the view that managers themselves clearly did not know what was going on. This view was shared by first line managers as well as non-managerial staff:

Last time we had [a business plan] all the people were made redundant. Management are saying they are not going to, but they don't know themselves where they are going to have to make cuts. (operator, pharmaceuticals)

Managers probably know as much about the future as me. It's all crystal ball stuff. (operator, chemicals)

The worst thing about working here is not knowing what the future would be – over-riding that is that people don't know if the plant is going ahead and where they are going to make stage 7, if the old plant is going to con-

tinue, if RDG is going to take off – there is … uncertainty. (shift manager, chemicals)

Internal Competition

The first line managers were also concerned that what was most important in determining the future stability and security of the site was not the takeover, but the way in which the site now performed. Many other employees realised that being part of a large company meant that sites were now in competition with each other for resources and products. Unless the site could win such resources from the head office its future was no more secure than it had been before the takeover.

*S*omething needs to happen. At the moment we're taking a very short-term approach. (supervisor, pharmaceuticals)

*A*s long as we produce the right goods, if we don't do that then … [the old company] only had three plants, now with [the new company] production could go to whoever is most competitive. (stand-in supervisor, pharmaceuticals)

Employees were very aware that future success depends on competition between sites as well as competition against other companies. As one pharmaceutical operator noted, 'within [the new company] there's a real fight among the sites, they're in compe-

tition in the efficiency league, and we're not doing very well'.

Resulting Employee Attitudes

There was also overwhelming evidence of a largely instrumental approach to work with the vast majority of employees citing pay as the only good thing about their job:

*B*est thing about working here is the pay, it's not the highest, but it's satisfactory. (operator, chemicals)

Pay was also a determining factor when it came to deciding whether or not to leave the company. While many employees expressed a desire to seek employment elsewhere, many were well aware of the lack of attractive alternatives. In pharmaceuticals, the women working in the packing area commented that the only alternative was working for nearby large supermarkets at greatly reduced salaries. In chemicals, many of the employees approaching retirement were just 'hanging on' until their pensions were secured. In industrialisation, given the type of qualifications (degree level) and the nature of the work, employees were in a national rather than a local labour market and could find well-paid work elsewhere relatively easily.

There was a significant lack of trust between employees and management and employees were sufficiently dissatisfied with their jobs to be searching for alternatives, but for the most part were unwilling to quit the organisation because of the relatively high levels of pay that they were enjoying and the lack of attractive, well-paid jobs elsewhere.

CASE ANALYSIS – THE ISSUES

In analysing the case you are asked to address the following questions:

1. How would you describe the management style of Pharmaco? How well do you think that Pharmaco's HRM strategy supports its business strategy?

2. What accounts for the differences between the views of employees in industrialisation, pharmaceuticals and chemicals about working for Pharmaco?

3. What, if any, steps did Pharmaco take towards implementing Greenhalgh's three strategies? Why did the company act in this way?

4. In what circumstances is a company likely to take steps to minimise the impact of feelings of job insecurity on its workforce? How important are job security, employee involvement and employee commitment to the successful introduction of new working practices?

REFERENCES

Brockner, J., Konovsky, M., Cooper-Schneider, R., Folger, R., Martin, C. and Bres, R. (1991) 'Interactive effects of procedural justice and outcome negativity on victims and survivors of job loss', *Academy of Management Journal*, **37**(2): 97–109.

Clark, S. (1994) 'Presentees: new slaves of the office who run on fear', *Sunday Times*, 16 October.

Daniels, K. (1993) 'A comment on Brockner et al.', *Strategic Management Journal*, 16: 325–8.

Dopson, S., Neumann, J. and Newell, H. (1997) 'The changing psychological contracts of middle managers in Great Britain: effects and reactions' in Livian, F. and Burgoyne, J.G. (eds) *Middle Managers in Europe*. London: Routledge.

Greenhalgh, L. (1991) 'Organisational coping strategies' in Hartley, J., Jacobson, D., Klandermans, B. and van Muren, T. (eds) *Job Insecurity: Coping with Jobs at Risk*. London: Sage.

Greenhalgh, L. and Sutton, R. (1991) 'Organisational effectiveness and job insecurity' in Hartley, J., Jacobson, D., Klandermans, B. and Van Muren, T. (eds) *Job Insecurity: Coping with Jobs at Risk*. London: Sage.

Guest, D. and Peccei, R. (1992) 'Employee involvement: redundancy as a critical case', *Human Resource Management Journal*, **2**(3): 34–59.

Newell, H. and Dopson, S. (1996) 'Muddle in the middle: organisational restructuring and middle management careers', *Personnel Review*, **25**(4): 4–20.

Robinson, S.L. and Rousseau, D. (1994) 'Violating the psychological contract: not the exception but the norm', *Journal of Organisational Behaviour*, **15**: 245–59.

Turnbull, P. and Wass, V. (2000) 'Redundancy and the paradox of job insecurity' in Heery, E. and Salmon, J. (eds) *The Insecure Workforce*. London: Routledge.

$\mathcal{C}$HAPTER TEN

TELCO:
MANAGING A
DIVERSE WORKFORCE

SONIA LIFF

IN THIS CASE STUDY WE AIM TO:

- LOOK AT the development and implementation of policies designed to manage diversity within an organisation

- EXAMINE the factors which have led to such an approach, the benefits that organisations expect to derive from it, and the extent to which they have been achieved in practice

- EXAMINE the extent to which such an approach frames an organisation's understanding of, and approach to, equality issues and hence EXAMINE the issues that arise for employees from such an approach.

Apart from the jobs they do and the qualifications they bring to the workplace, employees also have differences based on their position within society. Whether an employee is a man or a woman, from a particular ethnic group, has children or not, is of a particular sexual orientation, has a disability, enjoys working alone or in a team, finds it easy to work with computers or not may all affect what they want from employment and what they are able to offer. Some of these differences may also affect people's access to jobs and their progress within organisations.

ANTI-DISCRIMINATION LEGISLATION AND EQUALITY CODES OF PRACTICE

The way in which organisations treat their employees from different social groups is, in many countries, regulated by legislation. In the UK this framework is provided primarily by the Sex Discrimination Act 1975, the Race Relations Act 1976, and the Disability Discrimination Act 1995. The Sex Discrimination Act makes it unlawful to treat a woman less favourably than one would a man in the same circumstances (or vice versa) or to impose unnecessary conditions which women find more difficult to fulfil than men. The Race Relations Act provides similar protection against different treatment on the grounds of ethnicity. Recent legislation to protect those with physical or mental disabilities is similarly framed but in addition requires employers to make 'reasonable adjustment' to enable the employment of applicants with disabilities, say, by providing a special chair or adapted computer equipment.

Such legislation places controls on the extent to which employers are able to make distinctions in favour of some employees (current or potential) over others and provides a way in which individuals can seek redress. However, it does not provide detailed guidance on how employment policies and practices should be modified to ensure compliance. This gap was filled in the early 1980s by Codes of Practice devised by the equality bodies established under the acts (Equal Opportunities Commission and Commission for

Racial Equality); by the Department of Employment; and the professional body the Institute for Personnel and Development. These Codes consist primarily of guidance on how to remove bias from those HR/personnel practices relating to access to jobs and on how to monitor practice. Guidance on attracting applicants would, for example, include placing advertisements in outlets likely to be seen by a wide range of the population, ensuring school liaison activities target girls as well as boys and reviewing adverts and company brochures for sexually biased language or pictures of only one ethnic group. In many organisations such developments gave increased power to the HR/personnel function, reducing the discretion of line managers, and made practices more rule bound.

Codes of Practice also suggested ways in which organisations might go further in promoting equality, but without breaching the equal treatment requirements of the Acts which would make offering benefits only to members of some groups or introducing job quotas unlawful. These initiatives, commonly referred to as 'positive action', encompassed a variety of policies; ways to encourage more applications from non-traditional sections of the labour force; targeted training for those without normal entry qualifications; and support for employees with their out of work responsibilities through, for example, childcare vouchers or career breaks. Some organisations went further and included groups not covered by legislation in their policies on the same basis. For example, the BBC (2000) say:

*W*e are committed to equal opportunities for all, irrespective of race, colour, creed, ethnic or national origin, gender, marital status, sexuality, disability or age. We are committed to taking positive action to promote such equality of opportunity and our recruitment, training and promotion procedures are based on the requirements of the job.

Dickens (1994a) provides an overview of the UK equal opportunities approach and specific case studies of policies in operation (for example Jewson and Mason, 1986; Liff and Dale, 1994) provide further insights into its strengths and weaknesses. While some improvements have undoubtedly occurred, men still predominate in the higher levels of most organisations and in certain types of employment, particularly of a technical nature. Individual choice over training, jobs and ways of working (full or part time, continuous or interrupted careers) make it difficult to determine to what extent such evidence demonstrates the persistence of discrimination. Much higher levels of unemployment among members of ethnic minorities than members of the white population, even when matched by qualification, are more obviously linked to discrimination.

THE BUSINESS CASE FOR EQUALITY

Why should organisations pursue equal opportunities? The traditional answer has been derived either from an *ethical* framework where our values assert the importance of fair treatment, or from a *coercive* framework, that is, because the law requires us to do so. In the increasingly deregulated and competitive context of the late 1980s these approaches came under criticism. In particular guidelines were seen as overly bureaucratic and as such costly in terms of time and resources. Personnel was, in many organisations, being reformulated as human resource management and was seen as the responsibility of line managers rather than specialists. This, combined with an ever-more competitive environment in all sectors, led to a rejection of equality arguments based on moral or legal grounds. For equality initiatives to survive in such a context there was a need to make a *business case* (Dickens, 1994b), which explained to line managers how practising equal opportunities contributed to *their* goals and how they could make equality management part of the achievement of such goals rather than a separate activity.

So, for example, it became increasingly common to argue that it was important to ensure that women were treated fairly in the recruitment and selection process, not because the law required it or discrimination was immoral, but rather because a woman might be the best person for the job and thus an organisation which rejected this section of the labour market risked having a substandard workforce. Indeed, pressure to extend equality legislation to cover discrimination on the grounds of age was rejected by the then government on the grounds that it was unnecessary, since discrimination was inefficient and organisations already had all the incentives they needed to eliminate it in the form of their own business interests. These developments increased the tendency, already apparent, to marginalise the role of trade unions in framing the equality agenda.

These developments also combined to give a less central role to the human resource function for the development and management of equality policies. Indeed some questioned whether there was any need for, or value in, a distinct focus on equality. If such policies were seen as key to business success, it was argued, they should be pursued in an integrated way within other policies. As such, the role of equality as a central, strategic issue would be reinforced rather than marginalised. This approach is often referred to as *mainstreaming*, particularly within European Union documents. It involves moving away from specific actions targeted at, say, women and instead encourages policy-makers to think about promoting equality through general policies and measures at all levels. In the UK some government bodies at national and local level attempt to put this into practice by requiring each policy proposal or initiative to carry an 'equal opportunities implications statement'. So, for example, if consideration was being given to funding a new training scheme, part of the decision-making process would involve explicit consideration of the effect of such a development on equality.

CHANGING ORGANISATIONAL CULTURES

With a move to *mainstreaming* came an increasing recognition that providing equal opportunities involved more than the elimination of biased decision-making by managers. Issues as diverse as the language used in company documents, sexual and racial harassment, and styles of meetings were all seen as affecting whether individuals wanted to work in, and stay with, an organisation, and whether they were able to work effectively when they did. In implementation terms there was concern about senior managers' commitment to equality, line managers' ownership of the problem and approaches to dealing with it, and the ways in which equality initiatives were communicated to employees.

This language and approach mirror that adopted in other areas of HRM where culture and involvement were seen as key, such as the quality management movement. They involve a more sophisticated understanding of the way to manage change than the procedural approaches traditionally favoured by personnel. Specifically in relation to equality they recognise the need to change attitudes and beliefs as well as behaviour. While behaviour can be changed by detailed instructions being tightly monitored, the wider organisational behaviour literature suggests such an approach is also likely to generate resentment and sophisticated avoidance tactics. 'Opportunity Now', the business-led body promoting gender equality, suggests that culture change can be achieved through a virtuous circle comprising initiatives which demonstrate commitment, make the investment, change behaviour, communicate ownership, and share ownership (Business in the Community, 1988). Liff and Cameron (1997) discuss some initiatives which may be successful in changing the ways in which managers and employees understand equality issues and the measures necessary to address them. Any approach designed to create an equality culture, they argue, would need to

Challenge the assumptions which currently underpin equality approaches, in particular beliefs about the gender neutrality of current organisational practices and hence that women who are failing have problems and need help to fit in. It would also need to replace the current top-down approach to equality change with one that engaged commitment of those at all levels of the organisation, and men as well as women. (1997: 42)

LIMITATIONS OF BUSINESS CASE ARGUMENTS

Of course the increasing focus on the business case and the

declining role of specialists had a rather different consequence for some organisations. It has been difficult to convince sceptics of the 'bottom line' benefits from equality initiatives for a number of reasons. As with any organisational initiative it is difficult to isolate its role in the overall performance of an organisation. In addition change may be relatively long term and the costs of current inequality are unlikely to have been identified. These arguments may be particularly problematic in some organisations because of their competitive strategy or type of employee. So, while a business case for equality can undoubtedly be made in relation to managers or professional workers in organisations whose competitive strategy is based on quality or innovation, it is more difficult to construct one for small firms pursuing a cost-minimisation strategy using unskilled workers.

The most convincing case in the latter circumstances comes from evidence of the changing nature of the workforce. This shows that most of the growth of the UK labour force will come from women, many with dependants. Other demographic trends, such as evidence of an ageing workforce, many of whom will themselves have responsibility for elderly or sick relatives, reinforce the view that employers who want to tap into new sections of the labour force need to make sure that their practices are not discriminatory and that they are able to address the needs of such workers. Labour market composition is changing in most countries, although not necessarily in the same direction. In some, the changing ethnic mix of the workforce is the most significant.

MANAGING DIVERSITY

'Managing diversity' is a term that entered UK debates on equality approaches in the mid-1990s. It is still more commonly used in North America where it is seen as an equality approach of particular relevance to ethnic minorities. While it is becoming increasingly common in the UK, there is still disagreement about its meaning and the extent to which it differs from previous approaches. Champions of this approach stress its business focus, its integration within all activities and the responsibility lying with line managers. However, as we have seen, these have also become features of equal opportunities approaches.

One of the things which does seem to be distinct is the way these approaches deal with differences between employees. The traditional approach to equal opportunities (with its roots in UK anti-discrimination legislation) seeks to treat everyone the same (that is, without regard to gender or ethnicity). Managing diversity approaches, in contrast, recognises that employees are different and suggests that workplaces can benefit from addressing such differences rather than suppressing them. What this means for organisations is that they need to adapt to employee characteristics rather than simply expecting employees to fit in with the organisation's pre-existing practices. This highlights the need to rethink structures and cultures so that they fit better the characteristics and needs of all employees, in contrast to the maintenance of a form of organisation which suits the traditional type of employee but has some additional procedures designed to help others to fit in. One example of the latter might be whether jobs continue to be worked primarily on the basis of long hours in the office with, say, individual women negotiating to work part time or partly from home. The more radical alternative would be to restructure the way work is carried out so that everyone has flexible office hours which are compatible with a reasonable level of domestic commitment. Another example would be the approach taken to ensuring that appraisal was carried out in a fair manner. An equal opportunities approach to appraisal would focus primarily on auditing performance measures to see whether they have an adverse impact on members of some groups over others, and on ensuring that managers' assessment of subordinates' performance is not affected by their gender or ethnicity. A diversity approach would take a more radical look at what types of behaviour and activity are valued by the organisation to see whether these are more commonly practised by members of one group rather than another. While such characteristics may be associated with success for one group of workers, there may well be other ways of carrying out the job equally successfully (Chen and DiTomaso, 1996). So a male police officer might try to use his physical strength to control an unruly crowd, but a female officer might have just as much success through discussion and persuasion.

Business case arguments for diversity share many elements with equal opportunities approaches but they tend to stress additional arguments. These have included claims that diverse teams are more innovative than ones composed of homogeneous individuals and that non-traditional workers can reflect the needs of a wider customer base. In relation to this latter issue, the vice president of Pepsi-Cola has said that they have a clear business imperative to pursue diversity:

In our business it is about a share of your stomach. We want all of it, and we don't want that other company from Atlanta to have any of it. So from our standpoint the issue is how do we expand our share to be the greatest majority possible. And we can't do that by being exclusionary. (EOR, 1998)

Diversity approaches also place a strong emphasis on creating a culture within which everyone feels they belong and are empowered to reach their full potential. One aspect of this inclusiveness is an attempt to find policies which seem equally relevant to all employees. For example, career breaks have traditionally been seen as a measure designed to allow women to look after young children full time and still be able to return to work with the same employer at a comparable level some years later. But many other employees might value the opportunity to take unpaid leave for a couple of years without having to sever their links entirely with an employer. They might use this time to look after elderly parents, take a course or undertake an extended trip to Australia. The organisation could avoid permanently losing the skills of valued employees who might otherwise feel forced, or choose, to resign. Such an approach would also motivate a large number of employees who might previously have felt that the company was only doing things for women with children.

Beyond these common features, organisations have differed in the extent to which they retain a focus on the traditionally disadvantaged social groups (women, ethnic minorities, those with disabilities) or on individuals or more diffuse interest groups (Liff, 1997). The first of these is closest to traditional approaches to equal opportunities. It sees differences between people, in terms of their treatment and experience at work if not their intrinsic nature, as being primarily based on whether they are, say, a man or a woman. There is, however, a greater focus on adapting organisational structures and practices to the life patterns and experiences of non-dominant groups. This approach is often seen as building on equality approaches that have gone before. In short, equal opportunities facilitate entry into an organisation but managing diversity allows employees to be accepted for who they are, allowing them to work effectively and encouraging them to stay. This is in part also a reflection of broader social changes where, for example, it can no longer be assumed that all women will be mothers or all those looking after children will be women.

The second alternative is seen as the more radical approach. It argues that there are multiple sources of difference which are as important (or in some versions more important) than those based on gender or ethnicity. People are not defined by whether they are from a European or Asian background but instead vary along a myriad of dimensions including personality and tastes. These characteristics are said to affect people's work experience and need for training or support. This approach to managing diversity is strongly focused on individuals as the objects of equality policy and as such is in line with wider trends to individualise employee relations.

In practice, of course, distinctions are not so clear cut. The position paper on managing diversity from the Institute for Personnel and Development (IPD) (1996) would seem to be closest to the former position with its stress on the compatibility of new and old approaches. However, the IPD also puts strong emphasis on the role of the individual. In practice many organisations retain an emphasis on social groups but seek to extend this into new areas and stress individuality as well as group membership. For example, Procter & Gamble (2000) say:

*E*veryone at Procter & Gamble is united by the commonality of the Company's values and goals. Diversity is the uniqueness each of us brings to fulfilling these values and achieving these goals. Our differences are physical, such as race, sex and age. They also include less visible differences such as nationality, cultural heritage, personal background, sexual orientation, functional experience, position in the organisation, and others. By building on our common values and goals, we are able to create an advantage from our differences.

CAN DIVERSITY MANAGEMENT SUCCEED?

Apart from problems of commitment and understanding, equal opportunities has also been criticised as a strategy which is dependent on the opportunities provided by growth. It aims to achieve greater equality by moving members of excluded groups into positions within the organisation as they become vacant or new ones are created. Since this cannot be done by reserving positions, only by allocation on merit, change is likely to be limited at the best of times, and restricted during periods of stagnation or delayering.

At first sight, managing diversity seems to offer greater potential to enhance equality, even in a situation where there is little growth, since it concentrates on changing the ways those already in post are managed. However, it is important to recognise the problems of changing cultures, particularly via top-down approaches or in periods when the workforce feels threatened by redundancies. Circumstances in which the culture is likely to be most resistant to change are where there are strongly bonded homogeneous groups. So, for example, the police and fire services have proved to be in need of, and particularly resistant to, equality initiatives.

On the positive side, growing social expectations of fair treatment and for the recognition of individual needs within the workplace make it unlikely that this issue will go away. As increasing numbers of women enter the workplace, the view that workers can be treated as though they had no life beyond the factory gate or office door becomes increasingly untenable. In an ageing society, the desire to strike a different balance between home and work is likely to become more common. Business pressures will force many organisations to think about how to make real their claims that 'people are our most important resource'. In doing so they will be forced to think about the diversity of those employees and how to address this effectively.

THE CASE STUDY

TELCO

Telco is a major player in the UK telecommunications sector. It retains a strong engineering base but over the last 15 years has reorientated its business to give a much higher priority to sales and customer relations. The business environment for Telco is changing constantly. Two aspects are of particular importance. The first is the rapid development of the technology and the use made of it by both businesses and individual consumers. This has included the rate of diffusion of mobile communication networks and the growth and significance of the internet. The latter in particular has opened up the opportunity not just for more business but also for new forms of service provision. The second aspect of the changing environment within which Telco operates is deregulation. The opening up of the previously protected home market has led to a growth in the number of competi-

tors and hence to the need for Telco to defend its strong position. It has been relatively successful in this through a mixture of vigorous marketing, competitive approaches to pricing, high quality service and various initiatives to create a loyal customer base. Where Telco has gained has been through similar processes of deregulation worldwide. Telco's approach to expanding internationally has been via the establishment of strategic alliances with similar organisations already strongly established in a particular country. As a consequence Telco has developed a significant presence in European markets and to a lesser extent in North America and Asia.

Despite radical internal restructuring, Telco has sought to retain an image as a company that cares about both its employees and the wider community. It continues to consult and negotiate with recognised trade unions in the UK and has established a European Consultative Council. It offers high-quality training opportunities to staff at all levels and encourages them to obtain qualifications. Annual reports regularly assert the company's belief in the crucial role that its employees make to Telco's success and hence Telco's commitment to them. Employees' belief in this commitment has at times been put under strain by the extent of downsizing and restructuring which has been required over the years. During the 1990s alone the workforce was cut by almost half, although Telco still remains a major employer with a workforce of around 125,000. Telco has sought to reduce these tensions through generous financial packages to encourage voluntary redundancies.

Telco has also sought to promote an image as an ethical business within the community through both national and local initiatives. It supports a wide range of local and national charitable projects. These frequently have some link to Telco's business either in terms of the type of contribution they provide or through the type of initiative they are supporting. In this way such activities also play a role in supporting its products and extending its customer base. This is even more apparent in its support for government initiatives which have sought to extend the benefits of the internet into the public sector and the educational sphere specifically.

Make-up of the Current Workforce

With its focus on technology and engineering, perhaps it is not surprising that the Telco workforce is predominantly male. Indeed, with women making up over a quarter of their employees, Telco managers think that their performance is better than most. However, this figure hides wide discrepancies between divisions. Among engineering workers only 2% are female. Part of the improvement in the overall proportion of women in the company can be attributed to the fact that the numbers of staff in these grades has reduced by 50% in recent years, while other areas which are more likely to employ women have assumed greater importance. Even more dramatically, the lower operator grades (again traditionally overwhelmingly male) have seen a 90% reduction as a result of technical change. In sales, one of the areas which has grown in importance, women make up just under a quarter of employees.

Within the management grades Telco also feels that its performance in relation to women's employment is reputable compared with most companies it knows about. There are about 20% of women at middle management level and 15% at the lower levels of senior management. Above that the number of women declines rapidly – as it does for most companies. The chairman and chief executive are both white males as are all but one of the board of directors. The company recently conducted some research on both male and female senior managers to try to understand what, if any, differences there were and what might be the barriers to the future progress of women.

Telco also monitors its record on ethnic employment. As with gender representation, it feels that its achievements are creditable. For its establishments in large cities the ethnic composition matches or exceeds that of the local population. Again a more detailed examination would reveal some anomalies. The tendency of young people of Asian origin to take vocationally based technical degrees and other qualifications means that representation in this area is good. However, at management level representation is low, particularly of ethnic minority women. Some of Telco's products are specifically designed to aid people with disabilities. It has been keen to back this up with the employment of those with disabilities within Telco. It was pleased when a recent internal investigation revealed a number of cases where people with disabilities had been working successfully within Telco for a number of years.

Statements on Equality and Diversity

Telco has an equal opportunities policy statement which fits well within the law and recommended Codes of Practice. It goes beyond the legal minimum in a number of ways by including religion and sexual orientation within its policy, by making a strong commitment to find work for disabled people wherever possible and by drawing attention to disciplinary action which could follow from behaviour that could be considered harassment. However, its policy guidelines stress equal treatment, which ignores social characteristics such as gender or ethnicity, as the underlying principle which should guide employees' actions.

In support of this approach, Telco is an active member of a range of business-led organisations which promote equality and allow companies to compare initiatives and benchmark practice. One of these is 'Opportunity Now' which promotes gender equality, another is 'Race for Opportunity' which concentrates on ethnic issues. Telco takes every opportunity to promote its credentials as an equal opportunity employer through these bodies. It participates in a range of events and submits initiatives for consideration for awards. Initiatives relating to both ethnic minorities and gender equality have won public recognition through these means in recent years.

Alongside this approach, Telco is becoming increasingly interested in using the language of diversity. It particularly likes the way it seems to bring together issues relating to both employees and customers. In relation to the former, it seems to offer a way of building on increasingly individualised employee relations. It fits in with one of Telco's professed core values of 'we respect each other' and stresses the importance of allowing all employees to make their distinctive contribution to business success. With respect to customers, Telco stresses the way that diversity can help them to understand, and hence tap, new markets in both the UK and abroad.

Telco has actively used the concept of diversity as part of its communication with customers. It has asked how well its products and services suit different customers and has asked for suggestions from them. The feedback it has received has led to a recognition of the need to provide more guidance about its services in the main languages used by significant numbers of the UK's ethnic minority population of Asian descent. It has also made Telco more sensitive about the timing and manner in which it makes house calls to certain groups, through, for example, a greater recognition of the major non-Christian religious holidays. New technical developments to aid those with disabilities have been suggested. Customers with extensive domestic commitments have stressed the value of working at a distance for people in their situation.

The Management of Equality and Diversity

Twenty years ago the main role for the human resource function within Telco was to negotiate with the then powerful trade unions representing the skilled engineering and other manual workers. Along with other waves of delayering, which saw dramatic reductions to the number of levels of middle

management, the HR function is now organised very differently and has new priorities. It has been devolved largely to the divisional level, although it is still the responsibility of specialists. A relatively small group remains at corporate level with responsibility for strategic issues, formulating company-wide policies and carrying out a legal function.

In line with this, responsibility for equality is held in different ways at a number of different levels. A corporate-level responsibility for equality remains within the HR function. This is conventionally organised with separate specialists dealing with gender, race and disability policy issues. There are also advisers to deal with grievance issues relating to equality. In order to raise the profile of equality jobs further a small number of senior managers have had an equality dimension added to their other responsibilities. This is intended to demonstrate senior management commitment and ensure that equality issues are mainstreamed within all strategic decision-making. To ensure that this initiative cannot be dismissed as tokenism, the people picked for such roles are known to be committed to equality issues and their responsibility for this area is written into their job description on which they are evaluated.

However, most day-to-day equality issues are dealt with by HR specialists within the divisions. These people have a wide remit, with equality being only one of their responsibilities. Much of the detailed training on equality and diversity issues is dealt with by specialist consultants hired for that purpose. Telco is intending to carry out a further restructuring of the HR function. The number of specialist jobs in HR within the divisions is going to be drastically cut back. Instead, HR issues will be added to the responsibilities of line managers. This can be expected to lead to an even greater mainstreaming of equality work.

With the term 'diversity' now being more widely used within Telco, there are a number of initiatives springing up which have nothing, or very little, to do with the HR function. In particular customer services and community involvement divisions are finding the term very appropriate to describe issues that they wish to promote. Communications between different management areas are not always as effective as they might be. This has caused some problems in the sense of developing a coherent corporate line on diversity, but then diversity seems to be a flexible enough term to cope with these different emphases. For some of those managing equality initiatives on the ground this lack of strong central coordination has brought benefits. The scale of the organisation has meant that initiatives, which might have met with resistance if they had been more widely known, have been allowed to go ahead unchallenged.

Specific Initiatives

Telco has developed a range of initiatives to try to change the masculine image of its technical and engineering jobs and to attract women to see such jobs as a possible career. It participates in a national campaign called *Take our daughters to work*. Male and female employees in occupations where women are underrepresented are encouraged to bring their daughter (or another girl) of secondary school age into work with them for one specific day. Activities are arranged to show them around and give them a feel of the work being done. A linked initiative saw the production of a brochure, aimed at female undergraduates, celebrating the success of women within traditionally male jobs in Telco. Research had shown that one of the barriers to increasing the proportion of women in these jobs was that very few women did the degrees which had traditionally been seen as the necessary entry requirement. In response, job specifications were broadened and non-technology graduates targeted. Related initiatives were undertaken to target recruitment material at prospective employees from ethnic minorities.

For existing employees Telco has initiated a specific programme of training courses aimed at supporting talented women at different levels within the organisation and helping them to progress. These aim to increase women's confidence and help them to see how they can develop within Telco. It is hoped that this will reduce the number of highly regarded women who leave and ensure that Telco benefits fully from the contribution that these individuals are able to make to the business. Line managers were told that developing all their people was a key part of their jobs and one on which they would be evaluated. Strong pressure has been put on them to participate in a one-day training course on managing diversity and most of them have complied. Regular attitude surveys include questions on whether employees feel that their manager behaves fairly, promotes equality and values diversity.

Women staff have set up a network to provide support, information exchange and social activities. This is run by women themselves and events take place out of work time but Telco makes a contribution to the costs. Activities include a job share register, talks from women in senior positions and some more informal evenings when women across the company can meet each other.

The recent change in the disability legislation provided an opportunity not only to inform managers of their obligations but also to try to change attitudes for the better. A booklet was produced which provided guidance on how to interact with people with disabilities and what help was available to support their employment.

Reactions to the Initiatives

In terms of public recognition, Telco has won a lot of praise for its approach. Perhaps inevitably, reactions internally are more mixed. So, in relation to the *Take our daughters to work* initiative, the reactions of those

who took part were very favourable. There were also positive comments from some of the older male managers. One said: 'I had no idea so many girls would be interested in technical work. They seemed really bright – I hope some of them will come and work here when they leave school.' But the manager running the event also received a number of calls from men asking whether they could bring their sons in and some were quite irate when they were told it was just for girls. A number wrote to the in-house magazine whose editor decided to run a big spread on the issue linking it to recent media comment about boys' poor performance at schools. They quoted one employee who said:

My son really wanted to come and work here when he left school last year and wasn't accepted – I bet if he was a girl he would have been. I've worked here for 20 years and don't understand why Telco bends over backwards for girls who don't want to get their hands dirty and ignores boys who are really keen.

The increased numbers of women in management had also initiated debate. Some senior managers, who had initially been sceptical, have been heard to comment that they were impressed with the distinctive skills women seemed to bring. Their creativity and communications skills were seen as particularly good and very relevant to Telco's mission to expand into the global marketplace. In a similar vein, other managers commented that since they had increased the number of ethnic minority engineers there had been an improvement in the level of satisfaction from ethnic minority customers, and that these employees had also contributed to the development of some novel marketing initiatives. These views, and the company's detailed procedural guidelines, made the head of the equal opportunities policy group reasonably confident that selection procedures were fair.

On the negative side, a divisional equality officer reported that she had had to inter-vene during a selection discussion when one of the panel argued against the female candi-date on the grounds that 'she'll only leave in six months time like the last one'. Even more worrying was the behaviour of a group of male middle managers who had had quite a lot to drink at the recent Christmas party. They were heard loudly commenting on the likely sexuality of any women who would go on a women-only training course or a network event. When they had exhausted that topic they started naming some women who had recently been promoted, saying that the only reason for their success was so that senior management could say they had met Telco's gender targets. Another was heard to say, 'I'm getting a wheelchair for Christmas then they'll have to promote me'. A group of senior managers at a nearby table did not intervene.

Nor did the people that these policies were intended to benefit seem universally positive about what the company was doing. Interviews with women and ethnic minority people taking voluntary redundancy found that for some the 'white male culture' was a factor in their decision to leave. There had been grievances from ethnic minority men who felt that, while their managers were happy to let them work in predominantly ethnic minority areas, they were denying them the wider experience that they needed to advance. When the company contacted one ethnic minority employee to invite him to appear in a company promotional video, he refused and complained at length about always being the 'token black'.

A Clash of Cultures: Presenteeism or Flexibility

When those responsible for equality and diversity issues within Telco met to discuss progress they felt that many of the problems mentioned above were just transitional. Things would get better as the presence of different groups increased. They would become an accepted part of the workforce and would by their presence change the culture to be more positive towards diver-sity. One manager suggested that this process might be speeded up by taking a harder line against those resisting equality measures: 'one high profile disciplinary case and they would soon stop making racist and sexist remarks'. However, the majority view was that it was better to concentrate on initiatives such as the diversity awareness training which stressed links with business goals and rewarding those managers who handled diversity well.

They then moved on to discuss what they all agreed was a more complex and problematic barrier to equality. They had become increasingly aware that the culture of working long hours, pervasive within Telco, was a problem for many employees. An internal survey had shown that, while 80% of male senior managers had children, this was true of only a third of women at this level. The majority of men and women at this level say that work commitments overwhelm time they would like to spend with family and friends. A significant minority say that this would stop them seeking further promotion. Female employees at middle management level with young children, as well as those intending to start a family, are also saying that the working hours expected of them are unreasonable. Some employees with disabilities say that they would find it easier to work effectively if they were allowed to work from home part of the week or have more flexible hours. Although Telco has some formal policies to promote flexible working, very few employees had applied to work in this way. There had never been a tradition of providing or supporting childcare. It was known that a few small-scale initiatives had emerged at specific sites to create holiday play schemes. Management at these sites had reported that they had been valued by employees and that those with children in

the scheme seemed to work better as a result. There had been some discussion about introducing such schemes on a company-wide basis but senior management vetoed this on the grounds of cost and through concern that this might escalate into an expectation that the company would take on a wider responsibility for childcare.

As they discussed the issue, they agreed that there were two dimensions to the problem. First, the legacy of an overwhelmingly male workforce meant that there had never been any history of part-time or flexible working. Managers used to dealing with full-time workers with continuous careers found it hard to accept that someone who wanted to job share or have a career break could also be serious about their career. Managers lacked the skills needed to manage people at a distance, frequently voicing the concern that they wouldn't know if someone was really working if they couldn't see what they were doing. Employees were well aware of these views and only asked for flexible arrangements if they were prepared to put their career on hold (thus confirming the managers' views about their work orientation). But the problem went deeper than that. The second element was that the waves of redundancies and delayering of the management hierarchy had encouraged ambitious employees to demonstrate their commitment in ways that would impress their superiors. It seemed to be generally accepted that the best way to do this was to stay at work longer than your colleagues and to take home more work than them when you did go. In some sections this had reached extreme levels with e-mails being sent late at night or on Sundays to mark an individual's presence.

Those discussing the way forward agreed that this seemed to be much more than a problem of attitudes. Instead it seemed to call for more deep-seated changes in the organisation of work and in the organisational culture.

CASE ANALYSIS – THE ISSUES

In analysing the case study you should address the following questions:

1. How would you characterise Telco's approach to equality and diversity? How well does this approach fit within Telco's business strategy?

2. Can you construct a business case to promote more flexible working or address concerns about the long hours culture?

3. How successful would you judge 'mainstreaming' has been within Telco? In the light of this, what do you think will be the consequences of a further devolution of HR responsibility to line managers?

4. How successful do you think Telco has been in implementing its equality and diversity policy? Are the reported views of some managers and employees a significant barrier to full implementation? If so, how would you address this issue?

REFERENCES

BBC (2000) www.bbc.co.uk.

Business in the Community (1998) *Towards Culture Change: Examples of Best Practice*. London: BITC.

Chen, C. and DiTomaso, N. (1996) 'Performance appraisal and demographic diversity: Issues regarding appraisals, appraisers and appraising' in Kossek, E. and Lobel, S. (eds) *Managing Diversity: Human Strategies for Transforming the Workplace*. Oxford: Blackwell.

Dickens, L. (1994a) 'Wasted resources? Equal opportunities in employment' in Sisson, K. (ed.) *Personnel Management in Britain*. Oxford: Blackwell.

Dickens, L. (1994b) 'The business case for women's equality: is the carrot better than the stick?', *Employee Relations*, 16(8): 5–18.

EOR (1998) 'Workplace diversity – new challenges, new opportunities', *Equal Opportunities Review*, **78**(March–April): 18–24.

IPD (1996) *Managing Diversity: An IPD Position Paper*. London: IPD.

Jewson, N. and Mason, D. (1986) 'Modes of discrimination in the recruitment process: formalisation, fairness and efficiency', *Sociology*, **20**(1): 43–63.

Liff, S. (1997) 'Two routes to managing diversity: individual differences or social group characteristics', *Employee Relations*, **19**(1): 11–26.

Liff, S. and Cameron, I. (1997) 'Changing equality cultures to move beyond "women's problems"', *Gender, Work and Organization*, **4**(1): 35–46.

Liff, S. and Dale, K. (1994) 'Formal opportunity, informal barriers: black women managers within a local authority', *Work, Employment and Society*, **8**(2): 177–98.

Procter & Gamble (2000) www.pg.com.

ENGINEERING PRODUCTS: INTERNATIONALISING PRODUCTION

TONY EDWARDS

IN THIS CASE STUDY WE AIM TO:

- EXAMINE the way in which multinational companies (MNCs) restructure their production operations in the face of international pressures

- CONSIDER the role that MNCs play in the internationalisation of economic activity and the way in which many have sought to achieve greater international integration. In particular, it investigates the processes through which international integration takes place, focusing on the relationship between headquarters (HQ) and plant managers

- CONSIDER the role of the human resource (HR) function in the process of international integration and DISCUSS the implications of this for managerial and non-managerial employees.

The chapter begins with a review of the relevant literature concerned with these issues in MNCs, which is then illustrated with material from a case study of a multinational drawn from the automotive components sector.

THE INTERNATIONALISATION OF ECONOMIC ACTIVITY

In recent years it has become a commonplace to argue that there has been a 'globalisation' of economic activity and that this has led to convergence in business organisation and practices between countries (Sparrow and Hilltrop, 1994). One element of globalisation is that nationally distinct economic and industrial policies are being eroded by the influence of international financial markets and, in Europe, by the process of economic and monetary union (Mueller, 1994). Moreover, developments in information technology have vastly reduced the cost and time involved in communicating internationally, facilitating the growth in trade and the international subcontracting of activities such as data processing (Dicken, 1992). A further part of this process has been the growth of MNCs.

MNCs are powerful actors in the international economy, accounting for increasing proportions of employment, output and trade. One in five employees in the developed economies work for MNCs, while a further one in five work in their suppliers and, hence, are dependent on them (Ruigrok and van Tulder, 1995). Intra-enterprise trade within MNCs is now the single largest source of international economic exchange, surpassing international trade (UN, 1994). The sheer size of the largest MNCs means that their boards control a greater amount of economic resources than many governments, especially those in developing countries.

One motivation for firms to become multinational is to take advantage at the international level of the technological expertise that it possesses. Where this is the case, MNCs act as carriers of technological developments across borders, many of which are subsequently adapted by local firms (Dunning, 1993). As well as shaping the nature of technologies in different countries, MNCs can also shape the nature of consumer tastes. Through devoting large sums to advertising and marketing some multinationals, such as McDonald's, have managed to erode differences in tastes between countries and have subsequently expanded internationally on the basis of producing a highly standardised product. Thus MNCs have been one of the driving forces behind the internationalisation of economic activity.

Some commentators see the growth of MNCs as constituting the emergence of genuinely 'stateless' players in which MNCs are detached from the nation-state in which they originated (Reich, 1990). According to this line of argument, MNCs shift resources to wherever in the world market advantage dictates, develop a cadre of internationally mobile managers drawn from many different countries and are able to raise finance in international capital markets. However, portraying MNCs as 'stateless' is misplaced; relatively few MNCs, if any, display the characteristics expected of a company which is detached from the country of origin. Rather, the evidence demonstrates that most MNCs remain firmly rooted in their home base: few have more than half of their production operations located outside the home country; senior managerial positions are filled overwhelmingly by nationals of the home country; key strategic functions, such as R&D and the headquarters, are typically located in the country of origin; and finance is largely raised in domestic capital markets (Hu, 1992; Ruigrok and van Tulder, 1995; Hirst and Thompson, 1996).

THE ENDURING COUNTRY OF ORIGIN INFLUENCE ON MNCS

The concentration of the operations of MNCs in the country of origin means that they retain many national characteristics. One important distinction between MNCs relates to the impact of capital market structures on their behaviour (Marginson and Sisson, 1994). Whittington (1993) argues that the detached and diffuse relationships between shareholders and their companies and the key role of stock markets is, contrary to popular belief, specific to Anglo-Saxon economies. In contrast, in the Germanic economies banks are key stakeholders, having a close, long-term and interventionist role in companies, while in the Latin economies large investment holding companies, as opposed to stock markets or banks, are the dominant stakeholders. Furthermore, in Japan shareholders are interlinked through the keiretsu groupings in which there are mutual share-holdings between companies.

An important consequence of these differences is that in the Anglo-Saxon economies, termed the 'outsider' system, where shareholdings are fluid and takeover relatively easy, a primary concern of management is to stave off the threat of takeover through maximising the share price in the short term. Thus management in Anglo-Saxon firms are oriented primarily towards short-term profits and, consequently, finance departments have developed influential roles within organisations. In the Germanic, Latin and Japanese systems, all of which are examples of the 'insider' system, shareholdings are more stable and takeovers are less frequent, allowing management more freedom to pursue long-term goals such as increases in market share. This longer term orientation has resulted in production rather than finance depart-ments having the key role.

Since MNCs raise finance predominantly in their home country, we might expect the differences in the systems to affect their strategies and behaviour, resulting in variations between MNCs according to their country of origin. In particular, MNCs from the outsider system are more likely to view employees as 'disposable liabilities' and adopt a 'cost-minimisation approach to labour management'. In contrast, MNCs from insider systems can more easily pursue an 'employee development approach', seeing employees as 'enduring assets' to be invested in and nurtured (Marginson and Sisson, 1994). Indeed, the evidence is consistent with these predictions: whereas British and American MNCs have engaged in 'radical downsizing' and appear to be hostile to systems of employee representation, German MNCs exhibit a tendency to take a long-term approach to planning, training and investment and Japanese MNCs have invested heavily in greenfield sites in which there is a clear attempt to organise production along Japanese lines (Ferner, 1997).

Ferner (1997) suggests that there are four possible approaches that the MNC can follow in relation to human resource management:

- to adapt to the environment of the host country

- to introduce country of origin patterns into each subsidiary

- to develop their own 'hybrid' style across the company

- to be opportunistic where patterns shift from country of origin to host country and vice versa over time.

However, he notes that there is at present little evidence in Europe to suggest that the latter two approaches are being adopted in practice. Marginson (2000) argues that other factors are also important in influencing the design of particular HRM policies. For example, in relation to European works councils, his research reveals a significant business sector as well as a specific 'European' effect.

Therefore, while the country of origin effect remains strong, it is not complete. National differences in the way MNCs manage their labour are constrained by legal and institutional characteristics of host countries. The law stipulates to a greater or lesser extent how some aspects of the employment relationship are conducted, such as structures for employee representation and provisions for redundancy. The nature of labour market institutions, particularly trade unions, also constrains the freedom of MNCs, a prime example being structures of pay determination. In addition, as we saw in Chapter 2, national culture (Hofstede, 1984; Trompenaars, 1993) is often an important factor in determining whether HR practices are exportable. Indeed Ferner (1997) suggests that we are more likely to see some elements of HR influenced by country of origin and others influenced by the host country environment. These factors are set out in Table 11.1.

Table 11.1 Factors most likely to affect elements of HR	
Country of origin affects	Host country affects
Payment systems	Wage determination
Management development	Hours of work
Employee commitment strategies	Forms of job contract
Redundancy procedures	

INTERNATIONAL INTEGRATION IN MNCS

While the argument about 'stateless' MNCs is certainly overplayed, it is clear that many MNCs are seeking to achieve greater international integration in their production or service provision. Many MNCs have standardised their operations in different countries in order to market their products and services in a similar way internationally, a key part of this being the networking of production or service provision between countries (Coller, 1996). Moreover, MNCs providing business services have also attempted to develop greater synergies between sites in order to present a unified face to international clients (Ferner et al., 1995).

Accompanying moves towards standardising production and service provision across borders have been changes in the organisational structures of MNCs. Increasingly, they are moving away from organising themselves along geographical lines, such as national subsidiaries, towards adopting international structures that increase the degree to which they can 'capture the linkages across borders' (Porter, 1986: 18). In single-product MNCs these may take the form of a single management structure across the company, while in MNCs with a range of products international structures may take the form of international product divisions. The growth of these structures has forged stronger links between operations in different countries, facilitating the development of cross-border mechanisms in the HR function. A significant and growing proportion of MNCs have created mechanisms designed to bring together personnel and HR managers from different parts of the group. These include worldwide personnel policy committees, meetings of HR specialists and expatriate assignments. Marginson et al. (1995) show that these mechanisms are more common in firms with an international business structure.

A key question in the process of international integration is whether the creation of international management structures will be enough on its own to achieve such integration. Will plant managers from a multinational that was previously decentralised be willing to participate in mechanisms which bind them together with plants in other countries? In particular, will they accept as unproblematic a process that curbs the autonomy within which they work? This is an important issue for a multinational which is seeking to present a unified face to international customers and share best practice across its operations.

The literature suggests that the forging of internationally integrated operations will not be unproblematic. Edwards et al. (1993) see the balance between centralised and decentralised decision-making in MNCs as the result of ongoing negotiations and trade-offs between managers at plant level and those at HQ. That is, managers at both levels seek to preserve and maximise their own influence. Their own case study research illustrated the way in which managers at plant level have the ability to defy the wishes of the HQ: in the French plant of a British MNC the plant managers refused the demands of the HQ for redundancies to be made. They had the power to do so because of the expertise they possessed in the French environment – language, knowledge of French law, experience of the national culture – which made them indispensable to the HQ. Another illustration is provided by Szulanski (cited in the *Financial Times*, 1994) who found that subsidiaries may be unwilling to share best practice with one another where they perceive that doing so will reduce the competitive position of their plant in relation to other plants.

Nevertheless, as Kim and Mauborgne (2000) point out, involving senior subsidiary managers in the decisions that will affect them can be an important way of achieving integration. They found that where senior subsidiary managers felt that the process of policy development was consistent, fair and allowed for their input, there was greater acceptance of such policies.

One way in which managers at the HQ may be able to overcome the resistance of plant managers is to use countervailing sources of power. Developments in international communications, particularly computer networks, have made it easier for MNCs to compare the performance of their plants. Thus the HQs may seek to develop a degree of competition between their operations in different countries, and possibly to exercise 'coercive comparisons' between them, whereby plants compete with one another for future investment in what Mueller and Purcell (1992) term 'reward and punish' tactics in investment decisions. Indeed, there is a growing body of evidence to suggest that the HQs of MNCs are making increasing use of these comparisons in order to secure compliance with the wishes of the HQ by managements and workforces at subsidiaries. This is particularly the case in industries which are characterised by excess capacity, since in these industries the threat of closure underpins the comparisons, which is clearly the case in the automotive industry (Mueller and Purcell, 1992; Martinez and Weston, 1994). There is also evidence of comparisons being used to exert pressure on plants in other parts of manufacturing, particularly pharmaceuticals (Frenkel, 1994) and food (Coller, 1996).

It is not always possible for MNCs to bring pressure to bear on those at plant level in this way. Where production or service provision varies from country to country and those at plant level are experts in the local market, then the HQ will not be able to generate competition between its plants. Moreover, the nature of many industries requires MNCs to have a presence in the local market that they wish to serve, hotels being a prime example. In these circumstances, it is not possible for there to be internal competition between plants in different countries. It follows that the pressure on plants to engage in international integration will be less where the HQ cannot or does not exercise coercive comparisons.

The Implications for Managers and Employees

The process of international integration has implications for both HR managers and employees. HR managers at the HQ will be required to manage the personnel implications of integration. Uppermost among these implications will be the creation of international structures specific to the HR function which bring together managers from different parts of the multinational, enabling them to share information and reach agreement on the adoption of common policies (Ferner and Edwards, 1995). A further implication for the central HR function is that a key element of international integration is commonly the development of a cadre of mobile managers who move across the organisation on international assignments.

MNCs face a range of alternatives when it comes to resourcing management positions. The first decision to be made is on the type of 'international' manager that the company requires. Storey (1992) suggests that companies may use different types of manager for different purposes. For example:

- *Home-based*: someone who works in the company's home country, but has a focus on international markets and overseas competition

- *Multicultural team member:* someone who works on a series of international projects

- *Internationally mobile:* someone who undertakes frequent short visits to numerous locations, but remains loyal to and primarily located at HQ

- *Traditional expatriate:* someone who 'carries the corporate culture abroad' and spends lengthy assignments in a limited number of host countries, acting as the representative of HQ

- *Transnational manager:* someone who moves across borders on behalf of the company and is relatively detached from any single company HQ.

Identifying suitable managers, organising pay and expenses packages for those on international assignments and dealing with the problems that these managers encounter in settling into a new country are all commonly the responsibility of the HR department at

HQ. Research on the latter point suggests that a high proportion of expatriate managers experience difficulties in their time away from their home country (Tung, 1988).

Another implication for the central HR function is that it is unlikely to be solely staffed by nationals of the country of origin. The research on international staffing policies shows that several different types of staffing policy are currently pursued by most international organisations. The most common of these are:

- *Ethnocentric:* results in all key positions in an MNC being filled by managers from the country in which the parent company is based (home country). This type of practice is common in the early stages of internationalisation where a company is setting up a new business, process or product in another country and prior experience is considered essential. Other reasons for pursuing this approach are where there is a perceived lack of local managers with the necessary skills and the perceived greater ability of managers from the home country to coordinate subsidiary–parent relations and to transfer know-how from the parent to the subsidiary.

- *Polycentric:* arises where local managers are recruited to manage subsidiaries and are given local control of operations, but home country managers occupy positions in the corporate headquarters, so that headquarters' control (particularly financial control) is retained by home country managers.

- *Geocentric:* under this type of staffing policy recruitment, development and promotion are all based on ability rather than nationality. The best people are sought for key jobs throughout the organisation, regardless of nationality.

Perlmutter (1969) argued that as multinationals mature and seek to integrate their activities internationally they move towards a 'geocentric' approach in which senior managerial positions are filled on merit rather than on nationality. In practice, however, many European MNCs have favoured the use of ethnocentric staffing policies largely on the grounds that it provides the organisation with much greater control over local operations. This is particularly so where foreign business flows from large international acquisitions. If, prior to the acquisition, the new operation has been doing badly, then companies often perceive the need to put in 'their own people' to bring the business round. Furthermore, many European companies, particularly British ones, see the use of expatriates as crucial for management development purposes, with international experience seen as an important element of career development. This contrasts sharply with American and Japanese firms, where management development concerns do not play a large part in international staffing decisions.

However, ethnocentric staffing policies do have many disadvantages. It often takes some time for home country managers to adapt to their new location and during this period mistakes and poor decisions may be made. Home country managers are not always sensitive to the needs and expectations of host country managers who work for them, and the knock-on effect, in terms of the lack of promotion opportunities for host country managers, may lead to a lack of commitment, reduced productivity and high turnover levels. In addition, many companies are finding it difficult to recruit sufficient expatriate managers to meet their needs (Scullion, 1991). Given continuing rationalisation and restructuring, particularly in the UK, many managers fear that there will be no job to return to once the assignment is over, or that the job they are given will not be commensurate with the responsibility and autonomy they enjoyed while abroad. Increasingly, quality of life factors, problems of finding appropriate work in the host country for the partner or spouse of the manager, and concerns about children's education all play a part in rendering the prospect of an expatriate assignment unattractive.

The process of international integration presents both opportunities and challenges to HR managers at plant level. Many might welcome the opportunity to take on an international assignment, seeing it as a way of experiencing a new culture and increasing their promotion prospects within the organisation. Others, however, might be unable or unwilling to move for personal reasons or fear that it would be difficult to return to their previous position following an international assignment (Kamoche, 1996). The setting of common policies to the management of labour will also be a challenge to the role of the personnel specialist at plant level. Such common policies may represent an erosion of their autonomy; as we saw above, this is something that plant managers may seek to resist. Moreover, where standardised policies result in a departure from practices regarded as normal at plant level, such as the length of the working week or the introduction of a performance-related element in pay, it is likely to fall to the plant HR team to sell this change to employee representatives who may be sceptical (Ferner, 1994).

The main impact that international integration will bring for employees is to increase the competitive pressure that they face. As we have seen, managements commonly seek to generate a degree of internal competition for investment and orders as part of the process of achieving integration. Thus workforces will find their performance being compared with those in plants in other countries, exerting pressure on them to improve productivity and reduce costs. Those that compare favourably may be rewarded with new investment, enhancing their job security; for others the prospects may be bleak, with less new investment and ultimately the possibility of closure (Martinez and Weston, 1994).

THE AUTOMOTIVE COMPONENTS INDUSTRY

This case study is of a multinational company producing components for the automotive industry. This industry is one in which competition is primarily international: in most countries the product market is characterised by a high proportion of imports while production is dominated by MNCs. The 1980s and 90s have witnessed the expansion of Japanese companies into Europe and North America. For instance, Nissan, Toyota and Honda all now have operating sites in Britain. The performance of these companies has led many of the European and American companies to attempt to emulate their production systems and working practices, resulting in 'lean production' becoming widespread across the industry.

As well as seeking to emulate Japanese practices, the pressures of international competition have led the large motor manufacturers to increase the degree to which their activities are internationally integrated. Plants in different countries typically produce to common standards and often compete with one another for orders and investment from the centre. Currently there is a move towards international mergers, alliances and joint ventures which is having the effect of driving further integration. As the final producers of cars become more integrated, they demand increasingly similar components from their suppliers. Many of the component manufacturers are themselves multinationals and, hence, are under pressure themselves to standardise their operations across borders. This is the position in the case study firm considered in this chapter.

THE CASE STUDY

ENGINEERING PRODUCTS

ngineering Products is a long-established British engineering firm which for much of the 20th century produced fasteners for industrial clients. The company undertook substantial restructuring in the 1980s, selling off or closing many of its activities so that currently it has three business areas; automotive components, defence and industrial services. These business areas form international product divisions which are the primary axis of internal organisation, linking similar parts of the group across countries. The restructuring also involved expansion overseas to the point that half of the group's 33,000 employees work abroad; three-quarters of these are in Western Europe and most of the remaining quarter in North America.

The largest of the three business areas is automotive components, employing 60% of the group's workforce. The division is a first-tier supplier, dealing with several of the multinational final producers of cars, and is less concentrated in the UK than the company as a whole; Table 11.2 shows that

Table 11.2 The geographical distribution of sales and employment, 1996

	Sales %	Employment %
UK	21	16
Continental Europe	49	69
USA	21	15
Rest of world	9	0

only a small proportion of the division's sales are made in Britain, while an even smaller proportion of the workforce is employed there. Continental Europe is the base for a much larger proportions of sales and employment, with most of this being in Germany, France and Spain. The case study concentrates on this division of the multi-national.

In recent years the pressure from the automotive division's customers has become a central force in shaping how it manages its international operations in general and its international workforce in particular. The customers themselves have sought to standardise their methods of production and working practices through a process of sharing 'best practice' across sites. This has meant that, while the cars sold vary in minor respects between countries, they are produced in increasingly similar ways. One consequence has been that the components they purchase need to be of exactly the same specification in different countries. Since many of the first-tier suppliers in the motor industry are themselves multinational and in many cases supply the same companies in different countries, the

effect has been to persuade the components manufacturers to standardise their own operations internationally.

The Standardisation of Production Across Borders

The impetus for international integration in Engineering Products, therefore, came from the demands of its customers. Management at the HQ of the division have been faced with the task of integrating what had previously been disparate plants, serving customers in their own country and operating in a largely decentralised way. A key part of forging greater integration was to create management structures at the international level in order to bring together managers from different parts of the group, facilitating the exchange of information between them.

In Engineering Products there are several such structures which serve this function. The division operates 'manufacturing councils' which periodically bring together senior manufacturing directors from the plants to examine the processes which are adopted in each of the plants. A different structure fulfilling a similar function is the 'International College of Engineering', located in Germany, at which engineers develop and learn about new manufacturing methods. A further way in which the HQ has sought to drive integration at the international level is through the creation of an international cadre of managers who are expected to spend time on assignments in countries other than their own. One element of this has been the creation of internal consultants; these are managers who have been responsible for pioneering a new practice and who are subsequently given a mission of roaming from plant to plant assisting in the adoption of this practice.

In addition, the HR function has created its own mechanism designed to bring together managers from different sites to share 'best practice' and discuss common initiatives. This takes the form of regular meetings of HR specialists from different sites to discuss the implications of integration on personnel practice. These meetings have produced numerous instances of practices which have been standardised as a result, ranging from induction packages for graduates to problem-solving techniques. The evidence from the previous section suggests that, in creating international structures in the HR area, the company is typical of other MNCs.

It was established in the previous section that the creation of international management structures will rarely be enough on its own to achieve such integration. Plant managers from a multinational that was previously decentralised may not be willing to participate in mechanisms which bind them together with plants in other countries if this involves curbs on their autonomy. At Engineering Products, the key way in which the HQ of the division ensured that plant managers engaged in the sharing of best practice was the operation of internal competition for orders. Customer orders for components are increasingly placed at the HQ rather than with each of the plants and the HQ then makes decisions about which of their plants will receive the orders. This gives the HQ an important source of leverage over actors at plant level, who are increasingly dependent on the HQ. Decisions as to which plants receive new orders were informed by systematic comparisons of the performance of the plants in terms of costs and quality. A manager at the HQ described this process in the following way:

Decisions are made at the centre about sourcing to supply different customers so we will decide from which of our factories customers are going to be supplied. In the main, obviously, in the local market the local company supplies the local customer. But to an increasing degree we make decisions about sourcing which can entail moving production from one country to another for a variety of different reasons. Not only in terms of volumes but there is also influence over manu-

facturing processes now, so there is a greater coordination of manufacturing processes to make sure that the world's best practices are adopted across the organisation.

On occasions, the move towards standardising production generated differences of opinion between HQ and plant managers about the merits of a particular initiative. One such example was performance-related pay (PRP); the HQ was anxious to establish the principle of PRP in all of the division's plants and had been successful in doing so. However, the way it operated varied following discussions with local managers and worker representatives, so that the measures of performance, the proportion of the workforce covered and the amount of their pay subject to the performance measure differed between plants. Differences of views were generally resolved through discussions, but at times the HQ was willing to use sanctions to impose its way. One HQ respondent described what happens in cases where managers at plant level refused to accept that a practice favoured by the HQ should be introduced:

Well, if we believed they were wrong we would persuade them and then instruct them and eventually fire the chief executive. We don't get there too quickly but if they are refusing to learn the lessons that are available we take the action that is necessary to bring them into line. This doesn't happen too often because we employ very sensible chief executives, but we are directive to that extent.

Internal competition, and the power it gives the HQ, was thus instrumental in the process of international integration in Engineering Products. It induced managers at plant level to participate in the sharing of best practice across sites and to comply with the wishes of HQ in terms of the nature of the production processes and the way in which labour is managed. These developments had a significant impact on the work of both managerial and non-managerial employees.

Implications for Managers and Employees

The central HR function at Engineering Products had unquestionably taken on a more active role following moves towards international integration. A key feature of the function was the creation of structures which facilitated regular contact between managers from different parts of the division, while another feature was the management of international assignments. Taking on these responsibilities represented an opportunity for the HR specialists at the HQ, since it had raised the profile of the function, allowing it to become involved in activities seen as 'strategic' rather than just those that were 'administrative'.

One tension which the central HR function encountered was the balance between standardising practices and allowing variation between plants to reflect local factors. As we have seen, many elements of personnel practice were being standardised across borders, and the HQ was prepared to use sanctions to ensure that this occurred. However, in other areas, variations in the nature of the law, institutions and national cultures meant that differences in practices persisted. One example was the variations in the way performance-related pay operated; different arrangements reflected the expectations of both plant managers and employees concerning fairness. Another example was employee representation. In the American plants, there were no formal structures through which employees could be represented; the law did not oblige management to recognise unions and nor were unions influential enough to force management to recognise them. In the European plants, on the other hand, it would have been inconceivable for the company to avoid dealing with unions, given their well-established position in the plants and in some cases the legal support they enjoyed. Clearly, the central HR function had to balance the drive to standardise practice with adapting to local conditions.

For managers, one key implication of the international integration of the activities of the multinational was that progress up the managerial hierarchy was no longer confined to particular countries. The division has moved away from filling senior managerial positions with nationals of the country where the plants are located, towards a geocentric approach in which such positions are filled on merit, with nationality being of little importance. This has meant that there are more opportunities for ambitious managers to progress beyond the plant towards senior positions in other countries and at the HQ, which is reflected in the increase in the number of managers working in countries other than their own and in the number of overseas nationals in the HQ. While this creates opportunities for progression, it simultaneously imposes obligations on managers to become more geographically mobile. It is now a requirement for senior managers to be willing to spend time on overseas assignments, something that may not suit everyone.

A second implication for managers is that they are increasingly required to comply with the demands of the HQ and, hence, their autonomy is reduced. This was expressed by one manager in the following way:

It's increasingly a strongly coordinated effort from the centre of the division which makes sure that all our operating companies are working together to the same standards making similar products often with the same level of prices.

The result of this is that plant managers have less room for manoeuvre, something that some may resist. However, the existence of international policy-making bodies, such as the manufacturing councils, the International College of Engineering and specific structures in the personnel field such as regular meetings of personnel managers from different sites, means that managers at plant level have an input into the formation of policies and guidelines that operate at the international level.

For non-managerial employees there are also important implications of the process of international integration. Uppermost among these is the increase in competition between plants which arguably reduces the degree of security of each plant and, therefore, also of job security. We have seen how the HQ of the division routinely uses comparisons across plants in order to bring pressure to bear on plants that operate successfully elsewhere within the group. These comparisons, and the ability of the HQ to move production from one site to another, reduce the bargaining power of employees in each individual plant, having the effect of eroding potential resistance from employees and trade unions to change. Crucially, coercive comparisons in general and, in some cases, the specific threat of closure weaken the hand of unions in pay negotiations, resulting in downward pressure on pay and conditions.

Another implication for employees is that the process of integration has increased the extent to which they are exposed to working practices developed in a different country. Prior to the standardisation of production in Engineering Products, working practices were developed largely within each plant as opposed to elsewhere within the company and, consequently, were broadly typical of the country in question. While to some extent this remains the case, it has been eroded by the diffusion of best practice across borders. The key recent developments in work organisation have come from other plants, uppermost among these being a practice developed in one of the Spanish plants.

The high productivity of the Spanish plant had led the HQ to investigate the working practices in place at the plant. Visits by engineers and HR staff from the HQ led to attention being focused on one particular practice, a form of cellular assembly. This involved the reorganisation of the assembly of the product from a linear production line into a U-shaped cell. Under this new form of work organisation, employees were required to undertake a wider range of tasks than before which created a need for multiskilled operators who could work at any stage in the cells. Furthermore, under the cell structure, fewer people were needed for the same output, meaning that the workforce was contracting. The HQ staff were convinced of the benefits which would arise from implementing this practice in all of the other plants in the division and gave managers at the Spanish plant a mission of roaming between the other plants, spreading information about cellular assembly. The practice has subsequently been adopted in all of the other plants.

CASE ANALYSIS – THE ISSUES

In analysing this case you are asked to consider the following questions:

1. How would you describe the role of the HR function in Engineering Products?

2. In what ways has globalisation strengthened the power that the HQ can exert over subsidiaries?

3. What are the implications of international integration for the human resources department at the HQ of the MNC?

4. Why might managers in different countries resist moves by the centre of a multinational to achieve greater international integration?

5. What differences might we expect in the extent and nature of international integration in MNCs from other sectors?

REFERENCES

Coller, X. (1996) 'Managing flexibility in the food industry: a cross-national comparative case study of European multinational companies', *European Journal of Industrial Relations*, 2(2): 153–72.

Dicken, P. (1992) *Global Shift: The Internationalisation of Economic Activity*. London: Paul Chapman.

Dunning, J. (1993) *Multinational Enterprises and the Global Economy*. Wokingham: Addison Wesley.

Edwards, P., Ferner, A. and Sisson, K. (1993) 'People and the process of management in the multinational company: a review and some illustrations', *Warwick Papers in Industrial Relations*, No 43.

Ferner, A. (1994) 'Multinational companies and human resource management: an overview of research issues', *Human Resource Management Journal*, 7(1): 19–37.

Ferner, A. (1997) 'Country of origin effects and HRM in multinational companies', *Human Resource Management Journal*, 7(1): 19–37.

Ferner, A. and Edwards, P. (1995) 'Power and the diffusion of organisational change within multinational corporations', *European Journal of Industrial Relations*, 1(2): 229–57.

Ferner, A., Edwards, P. and Sisson, K. (1995) 'Coming unstuck? In search of the corporate glue in an international professional service firm', *Human Resource Management Journal*, Autumn, pp. 343–61.

Financial Times (1994) 'The difficult art of skills transfer', 18th November.

Frenkel, S. (1994) 'Patterns of workplace relations in the global corporation: towards convergence?' in Belanger, J., Edwards, P. and Haivan, L. (eds) *Workplace Industrial Relations and the Global Challenge*, Ithaca, NY: ILR Press.

Hirst, P. and Thompson, P. (1996) *Globalisation in Question*. Cambridge: Polity.

Hofstede, G. (1984) *Culture's Consequences: International Differences in Work-related Values*. Beverley Hills, CA: Sage.

Hu, Y. (1992) 'Global or stateless corporations are national firms with international operations', *California Management Review*, **34**(2): 107–26.

Kamoche, K. (1996) 'The integration–differentiation puzzle: a resource-capability perspective in international HRM', *International Journal of Human Resource Management*, **7**(1): 206–29.

Kim, W.C. and Mauborgne, R.A. (2000) 'Making global strategies work' in Bartlett, C. and Goshal, S. (eds) *Transnational Management: Text, Cases and Readings in Cross Border Management*. New York: McGraw-Hill.

Marginson P. (2000) 'The Eurocompany and Euro industrial relations', *European Journal of Industrial Relations*, **6**(1): 9–34.

Marginson, P. and Sisson, K. (1994) 'The structure of transnational capital in Europe: the emerging Euro-company and its implications for industrial relations' in Hyman, R. and Ferner, A. (eds) *New Frontiers in European Industrial Relations*. Oxford: Blackwell.

Marginson, P., Armstrong, P., Edwards, P. and Purcell, J. (1995) 'Managing labour in the global corporation: a survey-based analysis of multinationals operating in the UK', *International Journal of Human Resource Management*, **6**(3): 702–19.

Martinez, M. and Weston, S. (1994) 'New management practices in a multinational corporation: the restructuring of worker representation and rights', *Industrial Relations Journal*, **25**(2): 110–21.

Mueller, F. (1994) 'Societal effect, organisational effect and globalisation', *Organisation Studies*, **15**(3): 407–28.

Mueller, F. and Purcell, J. (1992) 'The Europeanisation of manufacturing and the decentralisation of bargaining: multinational management strategies in the European automobile industry', *International Journal of Human Resource Management*, **3**(1): 15–34.

Perlmutter, H. (1969) 'The tortuous evolution of the multinational firm', *Columbia Journal of World Business*, Jan–Feb, pp. 9–18.

Porter, M. (1986) *Competition in Global Industries*. Boston: Harvard Business School Press.

Reich, R. (1990) 'Who is us?', *Harvard Business Review*, Jan–Feb, pp. 53–64.

Ruigrok, W. and van Tulder, R. (1995) *The Logic of International Restructuring*. London: Routledge.

Scullion, H. (1991) 'Why companies prefer to use expatriates', *Personnel Management*, November.

Sparrow, P. and Hilltrop, J. (1994) *European Human Resource Management in Transition*. Cambridge: Prentice Hall.

Storey, J. (1992) 'Making European managers: an overview', *Human Resource Management Journal*, **3**(1): 1–11.

Trompenaars, F. (1993) *Riding the Waves of Culture: Understanding Cultural Diversity in Business*. London: Nicholas Brearly.

Tung, R. 'Career issues in international assignments', *Academy of Management Executive*, **2**: 241–4.

United Nations (1994) *World Investment Report*. New York: UN.

Whittington, R. (1993) *What is Strategy – and Does it Matter?* London: Routledge.

CHAPTER TWELVE

CONCLUSIONS: DEVELOPING THE NEW AGENDA FOR HRM

HELEN NEWELL AND HARRY SCARBROUGH

This final chapter aims to bring out the implications of our case studies for the way in which organisations should approach HRM. It will also point the way forward to a possible new agenda for HRM reflecting the kind of turbulent environment which has given rise to the challenges and problems described in our cases.

Having worked our way through the problems thrown up by the cases, we can begin to formulate some lessons for the way we view and practise HRM, and maybe contrast these with the conventional view. The first point highlighted by the cases is the sheer variety of issues encompassed by HRM, ranging from the development of teamworking to concerns about equal opportunities. This variety demonstrates the *scope* of HRM policy and practice, something which should make us wary of generic models of management and simplistic assumptions about human needs and motivations. Second, the cases also tell us something about the nature of the HRM task. One of the reasons for the shift from personnel management to HRM is the sense that many HR tasks have now been devolved to line managers. To underline this, it is clear from our cases that a wide range of managers are involved in carrying out HR tasks. The issue for organisations now is not whether such tasks should be carried out by line management or specialists, but whether all managers are fully aware of the HRM component of their job, and of the HRM consequences of their actions.

This ties in with a further point from the cases which is the need to develop a *holistic* approach to HRM. HRM is no longer the preserve of specialists and this makes it more difficult to coordinate HRM practices across the organisation. However, the need to do so is reinforced by the interdependence of different aspects of HRM, making it dangerous to treat issues separately or in isolation from each other. To take a specific example, in the Buildsoc case we find that the development of teamworking is not simply an issue of work organisation but is also intimately tied up with questions of motivation and reward, cultural change, management style and employee involvement. Likewise, the Telco case shows that issues of diversity are not only a matter of conforming to the law but also raise questions about the effectiveness of current ways of organising work and promoting employees.

In the first instance, the need for a holistic approach is simply because the individual employee's experience of work is itself holistic, in other words, the performance of the individual is influenced by a number of factors including their motivation, the fit between their skills and the design of their job, their commitment to the organisation's goals and so on. A company may enjoy state-of-the-art HR policies in one area, but if other policies demotivate employees or hinder their ability to apply the full range of their skills, employee performance is bound to suffer. The importance of the employee's overall experience in shaping attitudes and commitment should make it a benchmark for management decision-making in this area. This would not only ensure that questions of motivation and commitment are not left as an afterthought to financially driven decisions, it would also mean being more attentive to the legitimate expectations and concerns of employees, reflecting their characteristics in terms of gender, race and age. In an age when organisations are urged to address the diverse needs of different customer groups, it does not seem a big step to suggest that they ought to be able to address and manage the diverse characteristics of different employee groups.

The importance of the holistic approach is sometimes addressed by writers who speak of the 'HR system' in organisations. This highlights the interdependence of different elements of HR, something which we talked about earlier in terms of 'internal fit'. It is claimed that the development of an HR system can itself produce significant benefits for organisations, because all HRM policies and practices are pulling in the same direction. MacDuffie (1995), for example, finds strong evidence to suggest that the development of internally consistent 'bundles' of HR policies – linking reward, training and employee involvement – can provide an important underpinning for lean production systems. Of course, the idea of an HR system is an ideal rather than a reality for many companies. As our cases demonstrate, most of the time managers have to cope with HRM policies which have developed in a piecemeal way over a number of years, and where there are often inconsistencies or anomalies – different policies pointing in different directions. This does not negate the point about the importance of an integrated and systemic approach to HR system – arguably it even underlines it – but it does suggest that this is more likely to emerge when managers at all levels have a clear sense of purpose and direction in the way that they deal with employees.

HRM AND THE MANAGEMENT OF CHANGE

The difficulties of developing an HR system or of 'fitting' HRM strategy to business strategy are partly a reflection of the dynamic and uncertain environment within which organisations are operating. Consider two major shifts in the business environment which have taken place in the past decade. One, the move from hierarchical to process-based organisations, and the other, the switch from contracts of employment to contracts for performance. Our cases illustrate these trends and link them to a number of different kinds of environmental change including the impact of IT, changes in legal regulation and globalisation. Organisations need continuously to adapt and reinvent their management practices if they are to adapt and exploit such change. This has led to successive 'waves' of new management techniques being adopted by organisations. Among such waves we find the widespread adoption of concepts such as lean production and business process re-engineering (BPR).

One common feature in many of these new approaches is a tendency to neglect the importance of people in favour of new techniques or systems for production and service delivery. Lean production, for example, has been viewed as 'lean and mean' by many commentators who see managers using it to justify cuts in workforce levels. Likewise, even one of its champions has conceded that BPR became 'the fad that forgot people' (Davenport, 1996). Against this backdrop, it may sometimes be difficult for managers to sustain a commitment to good HRM practice. However, the need to do so is underlined by the consistent finding – remarkably consistent given the range of different situations involved – that HRM practices become more, not less, important in the aftermath of new approaches (Hutchinson et al., 1998). Certainly, new HRM practices need to be developed in order to support the new production arrangements, such that initiatives on quality or the development of supply chains go beyond merely cosmetic changes and bring about a genuinely radical improvement in performance.

*H*RM: DEVELOPING THE NEW AGENDA

One of the consequences of the growth of the 'knowledge economy' has been the perceived importance of the skills and creativity of employees in producing innovation and growth. As a result, HRM issues are increasingly regarded as central to the long-run strategic development of organisations. Whereas the focus of lean production and BPR was on efficiency and cost reduction, the experience of many leading organisations, especially from the high-tech sectors, suggests that competitive success increasingly depends on the ability to nurture 'core competencies' (Prahalad and Hamel, 1990) or skills.

This interest in knowledge and skills places HRM centre-stage in the evolution of the firm. Arguably, in some environments it redefines the relationship between HRM and strategy such that 'business strategies are adapted to fit the assets and resources created by … employment systems' (Capelli and Singh, 1992: 186). The argument runs that employment systems are the key to developing and appropriating employee knowledge. Kamoche and Mueller suggest that this means

*a*n approach for managing human resources which begins by retaining personnel, building their expertise into the organisational routines through learning processes, and establishing mechanisms for the distribution of benefits arising from the utilization of this expertise. (1998: 1036)

In other words, if organisations shift their focus from short-term cost reduction to long-term innovation, employee knowledge and skills are placed at a premium. From the delayering and labour shedding of techniques such as BPR, the wheel would turn full circle with companies becoming as concerned to retain skilled employees as they once were to discard them.

This view may readily be shown to be utopian in the event of another downturn in the business cycle or a shift away from the high-tech model of HRM. However, either way it does demonstrate one of the key points to emerge from all our case studies: it is no longer appropriate to treat HRM and business strategy as separate issues. In a world of global competition, rapid technological change and dynamic market forces, HRM is increasingly integral to organisational performance. Unlike other strategic drivers of the business, it offers no 'quick fixes', nor is it like other resources which are easy to measure and manipulate. On the other hand, in a global context of increasingly brutal competition, the organisation's employees and the way they are managed may ultimately represent a major and unique source of sustainable competitive advantage.

REFERENCES

Capelli, P. and H. Singh (1992) 'Integrating strategic human resources and strategic management', in Lewis, D., Mitchell, O. and Sherer, P. (eds) *Research Frontiers in Industrial Relations and Human Resources*. New York: International Industrial Relations Association.

Davenport, T.H. (1996) 'Why reengineering failed: the fad that forgot people'. *Fast Company*, Premier Issue, 70–4.

Hutchinson, S., Kinnie, N., Purcell, J., Collinson, M., Scarbrough, H. and Terry, M. (1998) 'Getting Fit, Staying Fit: Developing Lean and Responsive Organizations', *Issues in People Management*, **15**.

Kamoche, K. and Mueller, F. (1998) 'Human resource management and the appropriation–learning perspective', *Human Relations*, **51**(8): 1033–60.

MacDuffie, J.P. (1995) 'Human resource bundles and manufacturing performance: organisational logic and flexible production systems in the world auto industry', *Industrial and Labor Relations Review*, **48**(2): 197–221.

Prahalad, C.K. and Hamel, G. (1990) 'The core competence of the corporation', *Harvard Business Review*, May–June, pp. 79–91.

AUTHOR INDEX

SUBJECT INDEX